The Wild Idea Club

A Collaborative System to Solve Workplace Problems, Improve Efficiency, and Boost Your Bottom Line

Lee Silber, Andrew Chapman, and Linda Krall

Career
PRESS

Franklin Lakes, NJ

THE WILD IDEA CLUB
EDITED AND TYPESET BY KARA KUMPEL
Cover design by Howard Grossman/12E Design
Printed in the U.S.A.

To order this title, please call toll-free 1-800-CAREER-1 (NJ and Canada: 201-848-0310) to order using VISA or MasterCard, or for further information on books from Career Press.

The Career Press, Inc., 3 Tice Road, PO Box 687,
Franklin Lakes, NJ 07417
www.careerpress.com

Library of Congress Cataloging-in-Publication Data
Silber, Lee T.
    The wild idea club : a collaborative system to solve workplace problems, improve efficiency, and boost your bottom line / by Lee Silber, Andrew Chapman, and Linda Krall.
        p. cm.
    Includes index.
    ISBN 978-1-60163-057-5
    1. Creative ability in business. 2. Success in business. 3. Problem solving. I. Chapman, Andrew, 1966- II. Krall, Linda. III. Title.

HD53.S557 2009
658.4'036—dc22

                                                                    2008055439

If at first the idea is not absurd,
then there is no hope for it.
—Albert Einstein

Dedications

To Ethan and Evan, my two young sons who have wild ideas every day about everything, and yes, we have started our own Wild Idea Club.

—Lee

To my parents and sister, who've always encouraged and supported my ideas, no matter how crazy they seemed.

—Andrew

To my family, who always supports my entrepreneurial pursuits and creative ideas no matter how wild they are!

—Linda

Acknowledgments

Behind every big thinker are people who take their wild ideas and turn them into something tangible. For more than 20 years, that person has been my wife, Andrea. (I'm the big-picture person, and she deals with the details.) For the past 10 years, Toni Lopopolo has been able to decipher my scribbles and doodles and turn them into book deals; thank you, Toni. I must give a big high-five to my friend Doug Vance, who listened to me explain my idea for this book a couple of years ago and coined the phrase "Wild Idea Club." Good call, Doug. Finally, for the past several months, the people at Career Press have been fantastic. Without their support this book wouldn't exist.

—Lee

Thank you, Toni, for landing this book deal in a tough market. My appreciation also goes to Career Press for believing in the wild idea that became this book. Many thanks to Lee and Linda for our Wild Idea Club. And lastly, a big thank-you to all the teachers I've had in my life, from preschool to college, because I'm grateful for you more than you know.

—Andrew

To Lee and Andrew, thank you for inviting me to on this journey with you; your talents amaze me. To Erika Kotite, Chris Pitchess, and Janine McDonald, words can't express how grateful I am for your friendship and mentoring; your insights and ideas are priceless! To Neal and my circle of friends, thank you for being such great cheerleaders. To my clients, thank you for the incredible experiences and learnings; you are some of the most innovative and creative people in the world.

—Linda

Contents

Introduction
What's the Big Idea?

Great discoveries and improvements invariably involve the cooperation of many minds. I may be given credit for having blazed the trail, but when I look at the subsequent developments I feel the credit is due to others rather than myself. —Alexander Graham Bell

The definition of a Wild Idea Club differs depending on which group you ask. If you ask managers, they will tell you it's an extremely effective tool to encourage and enable employees to focus on solutions: When a Wild Idea Club is formed around a project or a problem (or just to generate more ideas), the members are employees drawn from different departments to work together to share their ideas and insights to solve workplace challenges, improve efficiency, and boost the bottom line of the business. The members think through their ideas and bring forward only the best ones with a practiced pitch and plan to make them possible. It's a manager's dream come true: With minimal effort, employees begin harnessing their collective creativity and skills on their own for the betterment of all.

If you ask employees, they will tell you the Wild Idea Club concept is a Godsend. Finally, someone is interested in their ideas (and they have plenty of really good ones), and they now have an organized and efficient way to bring them forward—and have them taken seriously. These same people now feel less like employees and more like entrepreneurs. They take the success of the company more seriously now that they have a hand in helping make it better. In short, they are engaged (and excited) about being a part of the process of improving the workplace and making the company more profitable.

No matter whom you ask (employees or employers), the bottom line is that forming a Wild Idea Club in your company is good for the bottom line. It's also good for things that don't show up on a balance sheet (employee retention and satisfaction, just to name two). Wild Idea Clubs can be started by as few as four people or as many as two dozen (although 15 is a more practical limit). The club meetings can last as long as two hours, but are best when kept to under an hour, once or twice a month. And they can be done in person, on the phone, or online.

By following the guidelines and examples set forth in this book, a manager will have very little to do—but will gain a great deal when the club pitches their ideas in a professional and polished manner, focusing on practicality and a plan. Giving your employees your blessing to form a Wild Idea Club is truly a win-win proposition.

The collective genius of a group is a powerful thing—when harnessed. In fact, studies have proven that organizations made up of teams outperform traditional bureaucracies. In many progressive companies such as Toyota, Southwest Airlines, Craigslist, YouTube, and Apple, the most important innovations come out of small groups, and account for a large percentage of the profits. That's where the Wild Idea Club comes in. It's all about helping employees and employers discover the amazing results this concept can create in the workplace. And because it is based on universal principles of human creativity and organizational thinking, it will work regardless of the occupation, organization, or industry.

Tapping into employee creativity requires a system. Brainstorming sessions and meetings that go nowhere, get bogged down in details, or lack follow-through are immediately improved by the implementation of a Wild Idea Club—and this book outlines exactly how to start and maintain one (or more). The manager who taps into his or her people's creativity by fostering a collaborative atmosphere will be rewarded with real results. Businesses that take advantage of this mastermind principle will see dramatic improvements in sales, service, and overall success. This is the edge companies need to thrive in the current (highly competitive) business climate.

Many companies—and the people who run them—believe the best ideas come from the top. There's no doubt most managers and executives have the education, experience, and expertise to come up with big ideas. But it's also true that the people in the middle and on the bottom of an organization often have a lot of great ideas to contribute—when allowed to. The landmark El Cortez Hotel (now condos) in San Diego was the first in the country with a scenic elevator that ran up and down the outside of the building, and the idea came from a janitor. Now more than ever, companies need new and workable ideas to survive and thrive. The power of the Wild Idea Club comes from managers harnessing the innate ingenuity and entrepreneurship of their employees.

If there is one constant in business it is this: There are always problems to be solved. Workers who offer viable solutions to problems rather than complain about them are an asset to their managers and the organization. The Wild Idea Club concept encourages solution-oriented thinking and initiative in people. It not only fosters new ideas that can propel a business forward, but is also extremely effective in tackling the common complaints within companies that never seem to get solved—one of the biggest benefits of this concept.

Ultimately, the purpose of this book is to help managers tap into their employees' natural abilities, so that important and breakthrough ideas are no longer languishing in their workers' heads. This approach to work-related problem-solving increases employee retention, because the office environment becomes fun and energized, and workers feel important. As a result they take greater pride in their work.

Using the creative but highly practical methods in this book, managers can capture their workers' creativity and turn it into real results. And because the Wild Idea Club concept is so simple, a club (or many) can be set up and maintained quickly. This book is a comprehensive guide to help executives, managers, and business owners do just that. The appendix provides an extensive list of quick tips to put the club principles into immediate action.

What company wouldn't want breakthrough ideas provided by its employees, with results ranging from dramatically increased sales and reduced costs to improved customer service and time saved (with less stress)? The Wild Idea Club fosters a more harmonious relationship between employees and management and creates a positive work environment—plus an improved bottom line.

Chapter One
A Meeting of the (Open) Minds

Minds are like parachutes; they only function when they are open. —James Dewar

Carole Scianna was the most unassuming person you could ever meet. She was 5-feet-nothing, 100-and-nothing (pounds), with a wardrobe consisting of nondescript clothing that had never really been in style. Carole was an administrative professional at a corporation so large they had hundreds of people who did what she did—but nobody did it better. And she was now noticed for being a force for progress and change in an environment where she and her fellow employees had to do more work with less time and fewer resources. It was almost impossible for Carole to walk down the halls of her building without someone stopping to congratulate her on something she had done. This wouldn't have been possible if it weren't for her manager, who had seen something special in Carole and helped her realize her full potential.

What set Carole apart from the other employees at the pharmaceutical giant for whom she worked? Besides being very good at her job, Carole cared about the company and believed in its mission (manufacturing drugs that save lives). She also wanted to make a difference in the lives of her coworkers. So what could a small, seemingly unimportant person working within the corporate culture of a huge company do to improve things for all involved (the company, the people working there, and ultimately the customers)? Facilitate a Wild Idea Club, of course. You saw that coming, right?

The idea to put Carole in charge of the first ever Wild Idea Club at the company came from Tom Fisher, a high-level, open-minded manager who was Carole's boss. Tom knew there were good ideas floating around the company (many of them Carole's); he just needed to find a way to capture them and start implementing the best ones, sharing the glory with all involved. When Carole came to Tom with the idea to form a Wild Idea Club it was a "perfect storm" moment—everything came together at the right time in the right way. They both smacked their foreheads and said, "Of course! A Wild Idea Club is exactly what this company needs, and we're the perfect people to do it." With Carole's energy and enthusiasm, plus her attention to detail and Tom's influence and connections in the company, the two began the planning process to bring their Wild Idea Club to life.

Tom laid the groundwork for the club—how it would work and who would participate. The members of the club ultimately decided exactly how to get the most from the meetings, but Tom provided them with a general outline from which to work. The first step was to find others in the company who cared as much as they did and wanted to make an impact by bringing about positive changes through ideation and implementation. Tom empowered Carole to begin recruiting the best and brightest people from several different departments within the company, and to propose their Wild Idea Club concept, which would bring everyone together to talk about solutions rather than complain about the things that bother them and make their jobs harder. Carole invited not only key people, but also lower-level employees who didn't otherwise have a voice in how the company was run. Everyone would contribute workable solutions, which would then be taken to the people with pull—their bosses.

What made the Wild Idea Club so appealing to Tom and the other managers was that *they* were also beneficiaries of the club's brainstorming sessions, gaining valuable ideas for improving everything from getting a better brand of coffee in the cafeteria and running a smoother office to innovative ways to serve the company's customers and sell more product—all without having to lift a finger. They were also creating an outlet for the frustrations their colleagues were feeling and providing them with a process to find better ways to do things. This would, of course, have a positive effect on employee morale and motivation.

Tom served as an advisor to the club and Carole facilitated the first meeting using Tom's general guidelines. They both believed that if a manager were present some members of the club might not feel as free to say what they really wanted for fear of repercussions. Tom quickly realized that the strength and uniqueness of the club was that its members had worked in the trenches, where they faced a whole host of challenges only they truly understood. Tom was very comfortable with Carole serving as his eyes and ears (something she did regularly anyway), while he remained in the background until the time came for the club to put forth their suggestions—then he'd be all ears.

At the first meeting, during their lunch break, the fledgling group discussed what their Wild Idea Club would and would not be. They all agreed there would be:

NO NEGATIVITY. The focus of the club would be on finding solutions to problems rather than dwelling on them. Instead of making it an open forum to complain and catch up on all the good company gossip during the meeting, they would leave time to dish the dirt during a "What's Up?" segment at the very end. This way they'd find out what's going on in different departments, because knowledge is power. But before the "What's Up?" segment, they would need to solve at least one workable problem. Also, as a rule, they would make sure any new members were positive, open-minded, action-oriented, and interested in making improvements to benefit both the workers and the company. The only exception would be to invite one glass-is-half-full person to serve as the naysayer when they were preparing to pitch an idea to key executives. This person would raise objections and try to punch holes in their proposals, so the group could be better prepared in advance. It wouldn't be hard to find a person who liked to see impossibilities instead of possibilities. But the Wild Idea Club's brainstorming sessions were only for positive people.

NO SUCH THING AS A BAD IDEA. Nobody should be afraid to share ideas, no matter how wild they are. To encourage wild ideas, nobody would be allowed to discount an idea before its potential was explored, and the more ideas the better. Carole was always known for being curious (though some called it "nosy"), and this would carry over into the club. They would take questioning things to the next level. Carole's favorite questions to increase creativity were: "Is there a better way to do this?" "What if we...?" and "What would Jimmy Buffett do?" They would then break down ideas for viability and build on the best one(s). The facilitator would make sure everyone's ideas were heard and appreciated. To make it fun and reinforce the concept that there was no such thing as a bad idea, a participant would receive a flower for every idea he or she brought forward. The person with the biggest bouquet would be crowned "Most Brilliant." They'd also go with the *Family Feud* courtesy clapping for every idea, even if the "survey says" it wasn't a popular one.

No homework. They'd meet in places where Internet access was available so nobody would have to say "I'll look into that" or "Let me do my homework and get back to you." The facilitator for the meetings would be a different member each month, and it would be that person's responsibility to make the announcement, agenda, and anything else required for the meeting to be a success. Everyone else would just show up with a positive attitude and an open mind. There'd be no homework, but members could do extra work to further the club's ideas. This included fact-finding missions—such as contacting their counterparts to see what it would take to get the approval or funding to push through one of their proposals.

No more than one meeting a month. The club would physically meet only once a month so it wouldn't become a burden, but they could hold virtual meetings as often as needed using various communication tools at their disposal—conference calls, e-mail, instant messaging, carrier pigeons, or whatever worked best. The only other time commitment was to take the agreed-upon solution and pitch it to the decision-maker(s) who could give them the go-ahead. Many suggestions could be implemented without outside approval, but there was a good chance some would need to be rubber-stamped by someone higher up, and the Wild Idea Club's strength would be in its numbers. This meant they would need to practice their pitch before giving it their best shot.

NO WASTING TIME. To keep the meetings tight, it was agreed there would be a leader/facilitator (they'd take turns), a scribe (someone to capture all the ideas and what steps needed to be taken), a timekeeper (to make sure they stayed on track), a clearly defined issue or problem to tackle, plus a theme and agenda for each meeting, which would last no longer than 90 minutes. Carole would commandeer a giant hourglass from one of her kids' games to use during the meetings, and the group would police each other for violating the preferred method of participating: Present your idea, make your point (and stay on it), and move on.

NO DROPPING THE BALL. No meeting would end without at least one agreed-upon idea to put into play and a plan to push it forward. Attendees would each be given a role that took advantage of their strengths and positions in the company to either avoid red tape or cut through it.

They further agreed to:

MOVE THE MEETING AROUND. Rather than meet in the same place every time, they'd meet at different times and places to keep the Wild Idea Club gatherings fresh and fun. They planned to meet one month at the shore during the summer and inside a roller rink during the winter. Other meeting places would range from different spots on the corporate campus to a nearby hospital to meet patients who are benefiting from one of their drugs and to get a different perspective on why their day-to-day work matters. Carole thought it would be cool to plan other field trips and maybe even meet on weekends or take a personal day (totally optional, of course) to visit other companies where employees were empowered and inspired. They could meet at night to watch *The Apprentice* or movies in which employees have an impact on the company (such as *Office Space*). They could also make a big deal out of members' birthdays and other milestones. Of course, they would celebrate in a fun and creative way any and all wild ideas the club was able to put into action. It didn't take much of an excuse to get this group to throw a party.

MAKE EACH MONTHLY MEETING, UNLESS DEATHLY ILL. To keep the club going strong, they would make a commitment to not miss a meeting for six months, to ensure consistency and build a strong sense of team. Everyone agreed, because they felt that the Wild Idea Club was the key to making important and positive changes that would benefit them. Plus, there'd be pizza. Being there physically would be a big part of it (including being on time), but being there *mentally* would be important too—no cell phones or BlackBerrys.

MAKE MEETINGS FUN. With all these rules, the main focus would still be on fun and creativity—kind of a controlled chaos. So they agreed that "ideation" (the process of forming and relating ideas) would benefit by making the meetings fun. This meant different things to different people. Carole felt what might make meetings fun (and increase creativity) would be unique warm-up exercises to wake up the creative side of the brain, as well as other clever ways to draw people's ideas out throughout the meetings. For the first meeting, the members would share (quickly) a little about their first jobs and their ideal jobs. Other members felt the title "Wild Idea Club" meant they would really go to town and dress up in costume, rent musical instruments, and order pizza. (There's that pizza thing again.) Because the Wild Idea Club would be a democracy and there would be no bad ideas, they would give each a try. They would also go to Michael's arts and crafts store to pick up some supplies sure to inspire creative thinking.

START SMALL. Carole knew the key to solving any problem would be to clearly define it and then break it down into manageable pieces. They'd begin by trying to tackle things they could get their minds (and motivation) around first, because it would be possible to make an immediate impact. Then they would branch out to the bigger stuff after gaining a couple of successes. The issues they'd look to first would be ones that could make it easier for employees to do their jobs—and put smiles on their faces. The other area where bigger wasn't necessarily better was in the size of the club. They agreed the best size was somewhere between six and 12 members, but no more than 15.

Then came the second meeting, which Carole led outside on a warm spring afternoon in the courtyard between two of the company's buildings. With the structure of the group agreed upon in their first meeting, they could now move on to their first problem—how to get the recognition they deserved for helping with the successful launch of the company's newest drug. (Each member of the club had worked nights and weekends to meet the deadlines the executives had set for them.)

All kinds of wild ideas were considered—an all-expenses paid cruise for everyone involved, a big bonus, a monument erected in their honor and placed at the entrance to the building, and more. After someone presented an idea, everyone tried to build upon it. Thus, the week-long cruise became a one-day team-building trip on the Hudson River (paid for by the company). The big bonus became matching money donated by the company for their AIDS Walk team. As for the monument...well, no one could quite build on that, except to say that the honored employee's supervisor would have to salute it every day for one week. But even when the "builds" got a little crazy, they were still beneficial in the fun and laughter they generated for the Wild Idea Club members. Never underestimate the value of a good laugh.

Lastly, they brainstormed an idea for T-shirts to celebrate their hard work that would read:"I helped my company launch its breakthrough drug and all I got was this lousy t-shirt." They thought it through (and envisioned themselves all getting fired), so they instead went with: "I survived the launch of PulmoMet."

♀ ♀ ♀

After a year of monthly meetings and instant messaging in between, this little group of go-getters had made a big impact on both the bottom line of the business and the enthusiasm with which they come to work each day. Believe it or not, the club members now actually *looked forward* to going back to work on Mondays—well, most Mondays. Their sense of involvement and contribution had grown exponentially, and their monthly meetings came with great anticipation and excitement.

As for the executives, managers, and supervisors, they were immensely satisfied with what Carole had created; one of the club's biggest boosters had also been its biggest skeptic in the beginning. This executive once referred to the Wild Idea Club as "the Waste of Time Club." Now he was anxious to hear what they'd come up with next. It helped that he saw the results from the group's collective efforts—which Carole had conveniently forwarded to him from day one, along with an article about how Toyota was well on its way to becoming the world's largest automaker as a result of creative collaboration and allowing employees to be heard. This same executive had then sent a memo saying ideas and input were encouraged from employees of all departments. (Hmmm, wonder where he'd gotten *that* idea?)

When Carole first gathered that group of coworkers from different departments to take advantage of their collective creativity, she knew exactly what she was doing—driving change the way she and the other employees believed would have the most benefit for all involved, including the executives and the corporation. By banding together, they were able to share their ideas without the fear of ridicule or reprimand, in an environment full of possibilities. It was intoxicating for the members of the first Wild Idea Club (and subsequent clubs— her company now has seven) to be able to share ideas and insights and then see solutions to workplace problems come to fruition, all because of the power of the people involved. The result was a group of energized and engaged employees actively seeking solutions that benefit the business.

And what about Carole today? We're glad you asked. Her self-esteem is through the roof, in part because she can now look around the campus of the company, point to things and say, "I had a hand in that" (the volleyball court), "and that" (every day was casual day), "and that" (a parking place right up front for the winner of the 'Idea of the Month Award'), and so on. Carole, who had seriously thought about quitting the company to start one of her own, now plans to retire there. She feels as though she is satisfying her entrepreneurial side with the Wild Idea Club, but still has her salary (she got a raise and bonus), job security (the company truly does need and appreciate her), plus benefits and profit-sharing (something she may not have seen if she started her own business). Finally, and most importantly, she is simply happy. Her job is rewarding and challenging, and the Wild Idea Club is an unqualified success.

The truth is, now more than ever, companies need new and workable ideas to survive and thrive. The power of the Wild Idea Club concept is perfect for harnessing the ingenuity and entrepreneurship of employees, to help them focus on improving all aspects of a company through ideation and innovation.

Workers with viable solutions to problems can now be seen as an asset to an organization—not just those employees with impressive degrees or big titles on their business cards. No doubt most executives have the education, experience, and expertise to come up with the big ideas. But it's also true the people in the middle and on the bottom of an organization often have a lot of great ideas to contribute—when allowed.

Now that you have a glimpse of one Wild Idea Club in action, what does it take to get your own going? How do you select the right people? (Some people just won't get it, at least not right away.) And perhaps most importantly, how do you get all this started with the blessing of the powers-that-be in your organization? Lucky for you, we've got that all figured out. So, if you're ready to get going and you choose to accept this mission, turn the page and learn how you can start to create something big.

💡 💡 💡

The appendix of this book is a point-by-point guide to starting and running a thriving Wild Idea Club. Use it to successfully launch the club, but also feel free to invent your own version of a Wild Idea Club based on the lessons learned from Carole's club and hundreds others like it, as illustrated in the following chapters.

Chapter Two
Ideas Wanted

Ideas are like wandering sons; you never know when they will show up.... —Unknown

When Lynn Andrews first went to work for a prestigious and prosperous clothing retailer during a summer break from college, she never would have guessed she'd still be working there 18 years later. Lynn worked her way up the corporate ladder by starting at the bottom as a cashier and holding almost every job except working in the café along the way to store manager. She also finished college and received her business degree—in seven years, but who's counting. That she is now in a position of power has everything to do with her work ethic, people skills, and her ability to brainstorm with others.

Lynn is the first to admit she is more left-brained (number crunching) than right-brained (idea creation). But this hasn't stopped her from being known as the most innovative (and successful) store manager in her region. The secret to her success is surrounding herself with smart, creative, positive people, and providing an atmosphere where all ideas are welcomed. Even the concept of collaborating with everyone at every level in her store wasn't her idea, but an approach she had learned from her favorite store manager years before. When Lynn was advancing through the ranks in the company, she often had to switch stores to get ahead. It was during one of these moves that she met Dave, a store manager and a genius at getting good ideas out of his people at all levels.

On her first day in her new position as an assistant in the human resources department, Dave came in and said, "Hi Lynn, I'm Dave. Let's get breakfast." He'd just come back from walking the floor of the store, where chatting with employees before the doors opened was his daily ritual. He also made himself available on a daily basis to listen to any ideas and insights from those in the trenches, which is what had prompted him to drop in on Lynn.

She was a little taken aback. The store manager wanted to have breakfast with *her*? "Come on missy, drop what you're doing, we're going to the café." Seeing her hesitation—she actually dropped her handbag on the floor she was so nervous—Dave said, "Relax. Haven't you ever had breakfast with one of your managers before?" Lynn stopped to think about it for a second. She hadn't actually. Dave noticed her wallet had fallen from her purse onto the floor. He picked it up and handed it to her, saying, "You won't be needing this, breakfast is on me. They know me there." Lynn smiled, and followed Dave out the door.

On the escalator down to the café, Dave put his hand on Lynn's shoulder. "You're part of the team now, and even though I'm the manager, I want to hear all about what worked in the other stores you've worked at, plus any ideas you have that can help us here. I'm not afraid of borrowing solutions from other stores in the region." They stepped off the escalator and turned to pass the cosmetics counter. "Lord knows, they are always stealing my best ideas," Dave said with a smirk. Then, he suddenly stopped and turned to her. "Oh, and Lynn, do share any good gossip you have." She laughed. And Lynn made a mental note at that moment: *If I ever become a store manager, I'm going to do the same thing as Dave.*

As they continued on, Dave pointed out a couple of improvements along the way, crediting the people who had come up with the ideas. "See those comfy chairs and the mini magazine rack next to the dressing rooms?" he asked. "That's for the bored husbands and boyfriends who are waiting for their women to try on armfuls of clothing. We're also installing a brand new hi-def TV that'll be tuned to some sports channel. I certainly don't watch sports." Dave pointed to a young woman shopping with a man wearing a Tennessee Titans jersey. "But the men who shop with our customers do."

Lynn had to ask: "What a great idea; who's was it?"

"One of our sales associates, Sandra O'Connor. No, not the Supreme Court Justice. She mentioned to me a couple months ago that she frequently saw women being rushed by their guys while trying on clothes, and it was costing us sales. So she suggested making the men feel more comfortable." Yet another couple with a guy wearing a jersey passed by. Dave nudged Lynn. "I think Sandra said she got the idea from a TV commercial where the guys were huddled inside a rounder, having a party while their wives shopped. Now, that's pretty funny. And she was half joking when she told me about it, but it seemed like a good idea, so we did our version of it—and it's worked!"

"Cool!" was all Lynn could say, while thinking, *My old store manager wouldn't even talk to the salespeople, let alone listen to one of their ideas.* Boldly she asked, "Does this store do more volume than my old store?" Dave smiled.

"We may be the smallest store in the region, but we beat the other stores like a drum. Our sales volume, sales per square foot, and sales increases throughout last year make us number one. I can't take all the credit, but I will. I'm kidding. Kidding! The truth is, what makes us the best is our people and—"

Lynn couldn't help interrupting. "Yeah, and you let your people become a part of the process, and that's not normal, believe me."

Dave waved his hand and said, "Yeah, well, the ideas for the coolest stuff, the stuff that makes this store truly fabulous, usually come from the people in the different departments, not me. The people I like to hire have a wide range of backgrounds, experiences, talents, and skills that I don't."

"What skills do I have that you don't?" Lynn wondered aloud.

"Well, Ms. Lynn, for one thing, I hear you're very detail-oriented." Dave gestured for her to go first as they entered the café. "And I'm not. Now let's get something to eat, I'm famished."

It didn't take long for Lynn to seize the opportunity to show she could be counted on for more than mundane tasks. Lynn looked up at the menu board. "We didn't have a café at my other store. Is there an employee meal deal here? "

"A what?" Dave asked, clearly curious.

"You know, like a couple of meal choices for under five bucks, just for the employees—one for breakfast, and a couple of options for lunch and dinner."

"Oh my God, I love it!" Dave boomed. "I'm making you a member of the café's Wild Idea Club right now."

Lynn looked startled; she had no clue what a Wild Idea Club was, and said so. Dave explained that small teams were formed in different departments—or around specific problems or projects—to brainstorm ideas and move them forward. The clubs reported to him and pitched their proposals.

Not knowing whether Dave was familiar with her entire work history, Lynn shared with him one critical point: "I've never worked in a café."

"It doesn't matter," he responded. "Your employee meal-deal idea is about keeping people happy, and a happy employee is a productive employee. Because you're in human resources now, I'd say you're qualified." Dave also pointed out a key part of his management philosophy: "I value ideas over experience at this store."

"That's great," she said.

"You'll see. I'm calling a special meeting of the café's Wild Idea Club for a week from today." Dave handed her a pen from the counter and said, "Here, write that down. I want you there."

That first Wild Idea Club meeting Lynn attended included employees from every level of the café—cashiers, cooks, servers, and the café's manager. However, she wasn't the only one included who didn't work in the café. There were other people from different departments (cosmetics, children's clothes, and customer service) at the meeting as well. In all, there was a total of 14 people gathered around a few tables in a corner of the café. Lynn was surprised the leader of the meeting wasn't the manager of the café, but rather one of the servers. Right away, she was introduced and asked to share the concept of a meal deal. Being the thorough person she was, Lynn had done her homework. She first pointed out that the store had more than 400 employees—a number that didn't escape the attention of the café manager, who couldn't help but grin when this was mentioned—and that most of them went elsewhere in the mall to eat. The reason: it was simply too expensive to eat at the café of an upscale department store on a daily basis. That's where the meal deal would come in. Employees could grab a quick bite for less than they could elsewhere, if the price (and selection) was right. Lynn explained how a similar program had been implemented at a competitor's store she'd worked at years ago, and how much the employees appreciated it. Then the brainstorming began.

Ideas were flying everywhere—and being duly captured by one of the cooks on his MacBook to be later e-mailed to everyone involved. Within minutes, they had a plan. They would keep it simple: five different meals for five bucks. The servers would poll people at the company to find out what type of meals would work best. The manager would run the numbers to make sure the possibilities would lead to profitability—or at least allow the café to break even. The cooks would experiment with a few meals and offer taste tests at the next Wild Idea Club meeting (which was scheduled during the lunch hour). The cashiers would design a punch card for the full-priced menu items so employees who didn't want the meal deal could earn free food by being frequent eaters. Lynn was blown away; in under an hour everything was coming together quickly and efficiently.

Lynn's role was to be the liaison between the club and Dave. Because the idea was hers, she would be the one to pitch the final version, but first she would run the rough idea by Dave to find out what he might want included—or not included. Lynn left the meeting charged up. She had never seen anything like this before. No wonder this store was so successful—as was Dave. Later, when Lynn briefed him on the meeting, he brought up a good point.

"What about drinks? Are they included?" Dave asked as he sipped his favorite café drink, an iced mocha. Lynn quickly scribbled a note to herself to ask the club what they thought about adding drinks to the mix—especially coffee drinks. As Dave pointed out, "We want people motivated, or is that caffeinated?"

After her first Wild Idea Club meeting, Lynn was added to the group e-mail list and was able to bounce ideas off individual members or the group as a whole. By the time they all met again, she was ready, and so was everyone else. As they were all up to speed through the e-mails that had gone back and forth, they only spent half an hour polishing up the plan Lynn would present to Dave with the help of some of the key members of the club.

To make sure they were ready for Dave's skeptical and cynical remarks, they spent the rest of the time trying to figure out what his objections might be, and writing down facts, figures, and a foundation to overcome them. The process of poking holes in their own plan turned out to be productive, especially because they did it while sampling the items from the meal-deal menu, and they adjusted some of the plan accordingly.

The last step in the process was to make a mock menu, as well as samples of the final items to share with some of their coworkers for feedback, which they recorded with a handheld video camera and later edited for inclusion in the presentation.

A week later, Lynn and much of the team served Dave samples of all of the items on the menu—which he thought were fabulous—while he watched the video they had produced, featuring comments from their fellow employees encouraging him to approve the plan. Lynn also shared with Dave how successful this type of program had been before, at a store much like this one. Following that, other team members stepped in to say a few impassioned words. Lynn then closed with the numbers—something she was very good at—and projected profits: they were small, but the company would actually make money. Both the café's and the store's volume would increase substantially. But the presentation wouldn't end without one final touch. Lynn had one of the club members come out with a freshly made iced mocha made just the way Dave liked it, while she explained that drinks would only be a buck extra with the meal deal.

As expected, despite the mocha bribe, Dave tried (and failed) to find the flaws in the plan. Then, after a few moments of apparent (or mock) deliberation, Dave declared, "I love it. Let's make it happen, people." And they did.

Never before had Lynn felt so excited about something related to her job. The employee meal-deal rollout and subsequent success was a high point in her career up to that time. She knew that the key to it all was her manager's open-minded approach to new (and sometimes risky) ideas. She had also become a big believer in the power of Wild Idea Clubs—and continued to use them as she worked her way up to store manager herself several years later.

☿ ☿ ☿

Just as Dave had done for her, Lynn made it a point to welcome as many new employees as possible to her store. One such person was Jose, a real estate agent who decided to sell men's suits at Lynn's store until the slow housing market rebounded. Of course, the retail industry was feeling the pinch of the downturned economy as well, but Lynn's store was staying ahead of the curve thanks to a culture of creativity and the innovation generated by several Wild Idea Clubs operating in her store.

During her breakfast with Jose, she asked him about his time in real estate, and he shared an idea with her: Almost all of his listings had come from referrals, and many of his clients who provided the leads had bought or sold homes using his father, also a real estate agent in the area. After his father passed away, Jose made it a point to keep in touch with these people; many were, in fact, now family friends or people he saw at church from time to time. He knew that remembering the birthdays, anniversaries, and other important milestones in their lives was what made him special—and led to a lot of listings. So, Jose wondered if the store kept in touch with its customers that way. Lynn assured him that every salesperson maintained a data base of current customers and contacted them regularly.

"But what about the customers from years back?" Jose asked. Lynn was intrigued by the concept of calling customers who had stopped coming in for one reason or another and trying to win them back...but how? You guessed it; by harnessing the power of a Wild Idea Club—or in this case, two.

Just as Dave had done years earlier for her, Lynn introduced Jose to the Wild Idea Club concept and made him a part of an existing group that consisted of some of the store's top sales-people and support staff. Jose was to make his pitch to his new club and together they were tasked with coming up with a way to contact old customers and getting them to come back to the store to shop. Lynn let her sales superstar, Claudia, know that Jose would be joining her Wild Idea Club and that he had an idea that could mean more money for her. Needless to say, she was interested, and agreed to hold a special meeting at the beginning of the next month, and pitch their plan shortly thereafter.

In the meantime, Lynn got on Skype to contact her own Wild Idea Club made up of her company counterparts in other parts of the country—some managing stores as far away as Hawaii. She checked to see if any of them had ever reached out to their former customers in an effort to win them back. Lynn heard back from everyone, but her inquiry got a lukewarm reception with varying degrees of skepticism and several stories of failure. Lynn was undeterred. She asked each of the other managers why they felt their efforts were met with failure and found out what *wouldn't* work, which was helpful. And the more she "met" with her Wild Idea Club, the more she was convinced the concept could work with the right approach. So she started throwing around some crazy ideas with her counter parts until a few of those ideas started to make sense. She told everyone in her club she would get back to them as soon as she heard from her in-store team to see what they came up with to woo back their long-lost customers from the past. Only a couple of weeks had passed when Lynn's assistant informed her that Jose had requested an hour of her time so that the Wild Idea Club could make a presentation later in the day. Lynn cleared her calendar, anxious to hear what the Wild Idea Club would come back with.

"Well, we have good news and bad news," Jose started. "Which do you want to hear first?"

"Hmmm," Lynn replied, "let's hear the bad news first so we can work through whatever it is."

"Okay, here's our problem. The database containing the contact information for customers from a few years ago is in a format our new computer system can't read, and nobody knows if there's a hard copy or where it is." Jose waited for a response, but Lynn just kept listening. "But, here's the good news. We hooked up with Kyle here from IT, and he thinks he can retrieve the data."

"Kyle, what do you need to solve this problem?" Lynn asked.

"Uh, time, and access to an old computer somewhere here in the store."

"Done," Lynn said. "Anything else?"

Jose jumped back in. "Oh yeah, we came up with a really cool concept that will blow you away."

"Well let's hear it!" Lynn said, unable to control her enthusiasm.

"Right." Jose looked around to find Jenny, then motioned for her to stand and say a few words. "Jenny's the one who came up with this idea."

The 20-something, petite blonde stood and nervously fumbled with her large poster boards. Lynn recognized her as an employee in visual merchandising, but didn't really know much about her. Jenny revealed her first board, which was beautifully illustrated, and said, "This idea isn't really mine, it's all of ours, so maybe Dean could come up and talk about the first part of our plan, and Tamara can explain the next part while I show the examples."

Dean jumped up, not the least afraid of speaking in front of a group. "Thanks, Jenny," he said before launching into his presentation, his enthusiasm (and drama background) on stage for all to see. "What if we did a special event just for our long-lost and longtime customers? It would be part customer appreciation and part special sale. We could do it after hours, have it catered, with live music and a fashion show, and give the people who come a special one-time discount on anything in the store." Jenny frantically tried to keep up with Dean, switching from board to board, one showing people sipping wine and shopping, and another depicting a runway with parents and their kids modeling the latest fashions. "I know this sounds like a huge deal, but we worked it all out. Tamara?"

Whereas Dean was a sales superstar in the women's shoe department, Tamara worked in customer service, and was very close with Lynn.

"Thanks, Dean. What we were thinking is this: the café can cater the food, my parents' winery can provide the wine, and we could have your husband's band play," Tamara said confidently. "They would be perfect for this. Plus, that way we'd have a P.A. system to use for the fashion show and to play music when the band's on a break."

Lynn was clearly impressed by the idea, but felt she had to try to find something she could challenge. "What about the fashion show?" she asked.

"Got it covered," replied Kate, the manager of the kids' department. "We thought it would be cool to do a fashion show featuring some of the families we invite. We could also use our employees as models. I nominate Dean as our emcee." Everyone laughed, including Lynn, and then Kate continued with more of the logistics and details. When she finished, Jose stood again.

"So, what do you think?" he asked.

Lynn smiled, unable to hide her pleasure. "Good work, everyone. This is all great, but how do you plan to reach our old customers, as many have probably moved by now? And more importantly, how will you get them to come?"

"Glad you asked," Jose said, as Jenny showed off a beautifully rendered invitation on her next-to-last board. "All we need is..." and Jenny put up the last poster board with a surprisingly modest dollar amount boldly drawn in calligraphy.

"You got it," Lynn said, relieved that this somewhat risky venture could almost come out of petty cash.

The next day when Lynn got back to her Wild Idea Club on Skype with the other store managers, they flipped. They all thought she was a genius—even if the event was a flop, she still reached out to her old customer base, and would reap the rewards from that act alone. Little did they know what this one idea (and the event that went with it) would mean to her store and her career.

♀ ♀ ♀

Just after loss-prevention locked the doors to the store—a little early to prepare for the gala—Lynn sat in her office with the door closed. She was wearing her brand-new black cocktail dress, holding a glass of wine, and wondering what the heck she had done. *This was a huge risk*, she thought. *What if nobody shows up?* (Kyle from IT was able to retrieve the old customer lists, but many had moved.) *What if we lose money?* (Even though they had pulled the event together without spending a fortune, they did close a little early on a Friday night.) *What if something goes horribly wrong?* (Lynn made sure to get all the necessary permits and notified the store's insurance carrier.) *What if...?*

There was a knock at her door. It was her husband, Dan, looking very dapper in his all-black outfit. "You better get out here," he said.

"What's wrong?" Lynn asked, as she chugged her wine, worried that things were off to a bad start before they had even begun.

"While I was setting up my drums, I noticed something I think you should see." He led Lynn to a window so she could see for herself.

It was an extremely long line of people waiting to get in—and it was an hour before the doors opened. She took a deep breath of relief.

Dan then walked with her to the floor to see how the set-up was going. Everything looked simply beautiful. Lynn had borrowed the event coordinator from one of the bigger stores in the region to help out, and couldn't believe her eyes. Between what Jenny's team in visual merchandising had done to transform the store and Kate's staging of the fashion show, Lynn was blown away. Actually, each department had done something special for the night, and everything looked amazing—and went off without a hitch.

It was a magical and profitable night. The attendance exceeded their expectations, but the café rallied and met the demand. The fashion show featured many customers and their kids, whom Lynn recognized, but hadn't seen in a long while. Dean was fabulous as an emcee and her husband's band had people dancing.

When the Wild Idea Club had gone through the old database, they recognized a lot of the names—some because they were famous athletes who shopped at the store. So they contacted as many celebrities as they could and invited them to be a part of the fashion show and hang out with the crowd. That turned out to be a big hit with the husbands.

When Lynn got up on stage to introduce herself and say a few words, she told the story about how this event had come to be and thanked every single member of the Wild Idea Club who made it happen, calling them all to join her on stage and take a bow. It truly was a "without whom this wouldn't be possible" acknowledgment and moment. Jose and his team were beaming—and not because they were buzzed, either.

💡 💡 💡

After all was said and done, sales were stupendous, goodwill was off the charts, and something unexpected happened: two new Wild Idea Clubs were born. As Lynn made her way around the floor to meet and greet all the old customers—some who went back to before she was even the manager of the store—she heard almost nothing but praise for the event. But she also heard some complaints: the reasons why many of these former customers were now shopping elsewhere. Some were very passionate and had stellar suggestions for how they could be wooed back. Lynn listened, and then asked several attendees if they would be willing to be a part of a focus group. All agreed. They didn't realize they were being asked to be a part of a Wild Idea Club, but that was a technicality. They were all thrilled that their opinions mattered—little did they know just how much.

At the start of the first meeting, Lynn hosted what she called a "bitch and moan" session. In a Wild Idea Club meeting there are no bad ideas, but in this particular setting, she felt no complaint was too "out there" to not be heard. One woman said she had been a customer since the store first opened more than 20 years earlier. She recalled how in the good old days she could park right in front of the store at any time of the day and walk right in. Now, she was forced to park at the far end of the mall and didn't feel comfortable making that walk at night. As she pointed out, "I'm not as young as I used to be, and this area isn't as safe as it once was." So she put the problem to the group—which was made up of both men and women, young and old. Lynn used several techniques to inspire creativity and out-of-the-box thinking, and by the end of the meeting, the group had the answer to the parking problem—valet parking. *Valet parking!* Lynn thought, *Why didn't I think of that?* But she knew the answer: sometimes the best ideas come from customers. After everyone had their say, and viable solutions were settled on, Lynn thanked everyone and promised her best to make all their ideas happen.

Keeping her promise would be harder than she thought. Valet parking, for example, wasn't as simple to set up as you'd think. One of the major hurdles was getting approval from the property management company. Her store was the anchor tenant of the mall, so she had some leverage, but the there were layers and layers of red tape to get through to make it a reality. Plus, the owner of the mall was a giant corporation, and this would be a precedent-setting decision. So Lynn did what she did whenever there was a challenge that needed innovative thinking—she started a Wild Idea Club and invited everyone, from the property manager to the vice president of her company, to attend. Not only did she land the valet-parking arrangement she sought, but the mall management even added a car-detailing service as an option for patrons who wanted to have their cars cleaned while they shopped.

ᵠ ᵠ ᵠ

Sadly, it was during this time that Dave, Lynn's mentor and friend, had died unexpectedly. If it weren't for him and his belief that everyone in the company could be counted on for a good idea (or three), she would have never made it this far. Not only did she turn her small (but wildly successful) store into a flagship for the company, but she was also recognized as the best store manager nationwide for her employee retention and productivity, and, of course, exceptional sales.

Chapter Three
There Are No Bad Ideas

A hunch is creativity trying to tell you something.
—Frank Capra

Most people are set in their ways by the time they reach their early 50s. But not Anthony "Tony" DelVecchio, which is amazing, considering his old country upbringing and 21 years spent working his way up the corporate ladder of a conservative office supply manufacturing company. But at the age of 52, Tony was forced to rethink everything after losing his beloved mother to a heart attack and losing his job when the company he'd served so well for so long let him go after being acquired by a foreign firm. His entire world was flipped upside down, and he had no idea what to do next. He was too young to retire and too old to start over at another firm in his field. His kids were concerned, and he was scared out of his mind. Since he was a child, Tony had talked everything over with his mother, and she had an answer and opinion for everything. Now she was gone, leaving him a little lost. So he turned to another strong woman for advice: his wife, Marie.

"Tony," she said, "You hated that job and it made you miserable as long as you worked there." It was the day he'd been laid off, and he looked sick. "Let's look at this as a blessing," she said. Tony nodded, but he didn't see it that way. Sure, he hated that the company had ignored all of his ideas throughout the years and was so slow to change that it cost him and some of his closest friends their jobs, but he couldn't overlook that he was able to provide for his family all those years.

"Tony, I know what you're thinking," his wife said. "But don't worry, we'll be fine. You'll be fine." Despite her reassurances, he knew he had to earn money, and fast. He had very little put away and his monthly expenses weren't insignificant. He felt too proud to collect unemployment, but he would if he absolutely had to.

The next morning Tony awoke automatically at 5:15 a.m., but for the first time in years he had no idea what he would do with the rest of his day. He went outside to grab the morning paper with plans to scan the help-wanted ads to see what was out there for a 52-year-old unemployed salesman—until he saw the box on the coffee table. It was wrapped beautifully in gold foil paper with a blue bow on top. He searched for a card, but found none. The girls were both away at college and it was just him and Marie. Could the gift be for her? His curiosity was killing him so he carefully unwrapped the package. When Tony reached inside and pulled out the "gift," he knew exactly who it was for, and who it was from.

"I see you opened your present," Marie said as she entered the kitchen and grabbed a cup of coffee.

"Where'd ya find it?" Tony asked.

"Right where you left it, in the table beside the bed."

Tony flipped through the pages of his "Idea Journal," abandoned so many years ago. He was so caught up in his job that he had forgotten all about the wild ideas he'd come up with throughout the years. "Did you look through it?" Tony asked.

"I did."

There was a long pause until Tony pleaded, "And?"

"And I think you have a very active imagination," she said, stringing him along.

"Is this a bad thing?" Tony wanted to know.

"It was, when you worked for a company that discourages creative thinking and fears change. But now that you don't work there, it's a great thing."

"What do you mean?"

"What I mean is," Marie said as she sat down next to him, "I think it's time we start a business."

Tony was floored. His mother would have screamed at the both of them for even saying the words out loud. She believed you got a job and stuck with it until you retired—which Tony had intended to do. Starting your own business was far too risky a venture for a DelVecchio. As his mother's words rattled around in his head, Tony turned to his wife and said, "I don't know, Marie. Don't you think I should look for another job? We have the kids to think about."

"Exactly. That's why we should do this. We do it for them," she said, gripping his arm. "Don't you see? We *have* to think about our future, and our kids' futures, and the best way to do that is to start our own business and build it up so we can sell it or pass it on to the kids." Marie opened Tony's old Idea Journal and turned to a page she'd previously marked with a sticky note. "There are a lot of really good ideas in here, but this is the best one." She turned the journal around so Tony could see the diagrams and sketches of a business he'd envisioned years ago. It was even something his mother *might* have approved of. But...

"What do I know about pizza? What do I know about running a business for that matter?" he wondered aloud as he looked over his notes.

"Tony, you spent *21 years* working for a business that did almost everything wrong, so at the very least you know how *not* to run a business. That's more than most people can say. Plus, you're good with people, and a natural salesman." Tony thought about it, and Marie was only half right. His former employer wasn't always so risk-averse and slow to change. Tony had been there during the glory days too.

Tony was hired to work in the warehouse. Being in shipping and receiving gave him a good idea of what was selling as he witnessed the intense growth of the company. It struggled to meet demand, but ultimately expanded to include nearly 900 products, with sales in excess of $60 million and more than 200 employees. By 1978, Tony's success and experience in the warehouse (and his gregarious personality) led to a promotion as an outside salesman—just in time to see the business begin its downward slide.

Despite a decrease in sales, the company had expanded to a facility four times the size of their previous location, taking on an incredible amount of debt. This might have been okay if they had seen the signs. One clear signal that times were changing was the coming of the Information Age. Tony had pleaded with his boss to adapt and change to the coming shift in the way his customers were managing information. The new "paperless society" was not going to be good for a company that produced paper products. Tony had several suggestions that would have taken advantage of the impact computers were beginning to have, but his ideas fell on deaf ears. The owner— and the company as a whole—was extremely proud of its heritage, and got caught looking back instead of ahead as several product lines quickly became obsolete. The company also missed the boat by not going global and taking advantage of expanding markets in Europe, Asia, and South America. By this time, many of the company's key people jumped ship and saw the sinking sales as a sign of even tougher times ahead. This opened up a position for Tony, who took on the title of national sales manager.

In his new role, Tony presented ideas for new and improved products and packaging, which had become outdated and drab. Once again, the owner chose to "stick with what worked." But things weren't working, and Tony was forced to put in longer hours for less pay. The stress took its toll on Tony, but it claimed the life of the owner. "The Old Man," as he was affectionately referred to, had been working seven days a week desperately trying to turn things around, but died of a massive heart attack— at his desk, no less. The business passed to his son and daughter, who took over a company deeply in debt and facing its greatest challenge to date—the consolidation of office supply retailers.

These super-stores duplicated and sold many of the same things Tony's sales force was trying to sell—only they did it for a lot less. Although most office supply manufacturers moved production overseas (or to Mexico) to reduce overhead (something Tony had suggested himself), his employer failed to act, in part because they had just bought the new building to handle manufacturing and assembly. Now, not only was there a decrease in demand for the company's key product lines, but their customer base also shrank dramatically while their cost of goods soared. Tony still had hope the business could be saved, and offered several solutions, but it was too little, too late, and the siblings sold the company for cash to a competitor to cover their debts. Tony stayed on during the transition, but the new owners gutted the company and cut Tony (and everyone else) before moving manufacturing to China.

Maybe the most frustrating aspect of what happened was the fact that it could have been prevented. The mindset at the company had always been that new ideas are bad, which clashed with his personal philosophy that there *are* no bad ideas. For years, he'd heard the same rhetoric from his various bosses: some variation of "We've always done it that way and it's worked." The problem was, it wasn't true. The company had started with next to nothing and a single product, and grew in the beginning by adapting to the needs of the market. Somewhere along the way the owners and executives grew complacent and rested on their laurels, taking the seemingly safe route. To make matters worse, success went to the heads of those in charge, who thought they knew more than everyone—especially the employees.

Now, Tony couldn't change the past, but he could certainly use what he had learned in order to build his own business on the principle that good ideas can come from anyone and are everywhere—if you simply pay attention and listen. And that's what he would do.

While Tony was reminiscing, Marie was doing her best to get his attention. "Earth to Tony."

"Sorry. I was just thinking about what you said about knowing a lot about how a company can crash and burn. It's true. I've seen it all, and I've learned a lot, like—"

"Like you should trust your ideas," Marie said.

"Yup."

"And I happen to agree with you—for once." She smiled to make sure he knew she was joking and gave him a playful nudge with her elbow. "In fact, I think your idea about opening an authentic Italian pizza place is a great one. Everyone knows your mother made the best pizza on the planet. People will pay for pizza like that—trust me."

And Marie was right.

Since that discussion at the kitchen table in 1989, Tony and Marie (along with their family) built a very profitable pizza-based business by embracing their own ideas and encouraging (and implementing) the ideas of everyone else—employees, customers, vendors, family, and friends. Tony talked to as many people as possible, and also read everything he could get his hands on about business.

It all began with an idea club consisting of two members: Tony and Marie. The first thing they did was to bounce ideas back and forth before deciding to divide and conquer...and eat. Tony visited as many pizza places as possible looking for ideas to add to his own. While he was there he always sampled a slice (or three) of the place's pizza. So far, none came close to his mom's special recipe, and not one incorporated his idea of gourmet pizza and pasta delivered to your home. Marie was testing her version of the family recipe on everyone—friends, neighbors, and Tony—all the while gaining valuable feedback along the way. As a former salesman, Tony was quite a talker, and back in the late '80s you usually were able to meet the owners of any pizza place because they were there working it. Little did they know that the man so interested in their business was also intent on starting one of his own.

It was during one of his fact-finding/taste-testing missions that Tony met a widow who owned a small but popular pizza place at the end of town. Now that her husband was gone, she desperately wanted to move to California to be with her children, but felt that she owed it to her loyal patrons (many of whom had been eating there for two generations) to keep it running. She may have been highly motivated to move to a warmer climate and anxious to be near her family, but she wasn't going to give the business away—far from it. In fact, she wanted to recoup the cost of her recently replaced equipment and capitalize on her loyal customers by factoring this base into the sales price. And she insisted she would stay for a month or two to show the new owners the ropes...for a fee. Marie took a long look at the books and found the business was making good money, and it had been for years. Even with the demands of the current owner, it was still a good deal. Tony knew it was cheaper to purchase the place than to start a restaurant from scratch, but the asking price was much more than the cash-strapped DelVecchios could get their hands on. So they introduced the widow to a concept she'd never heard of: the Wild Idea Club.

At the first meeting, Tony, always the salesman, pointed out the positives. She wanted to sell them the business, and they wanted to buy it, but both had their price and they were sticking to it. It was time to get creative. Tony and Marie were able to raise most of the money by hawking anything that wasn't a necessity—including some odds and ends such as Marie's jewelry and 10 years' worth of office supply samples. The rest was worked out through some very creative financing with the current owner. Tony was an active member in several civic associations in town, and he made a deal to trade a lifetime supply (or 10 years, whichever came first) of pizza to a travel agent in exchange for a first-class airline ticket to San Diego—which the owner accepted as part of the payment. He did the same for several other services to save money. He also planned to introduce a pre-paid pizza plan and a pizza club such that people would be charged an upfront fee to get huge savings throughout a one-year period. In the end, they used several unorthodox ideas to buy the business and have enough left over to build it into the kind of place Tony had dreamed about so many years ago.

Seeing the power of putting people's heads together, Tony and Marie expanded their Wild Idea Club to include their kids, their neighbors, and anyone else who could be counted on to bring something new and unique to the table. Then they formed an official Wild Idea Club with the employees—all three of them. These informal brainstorming sessions were almost always held over pizza or pasta, and Tony would usually start these sessions with the phrase "What if we..." and then blurt out a crazy idea. Or he would say to an employee or a customer, "If you were in charge, what would you do differently?" People could then say anything they wanted or add on to the idea or come up with one of their own. Tony was always talking to patrons and encouraging them to share their thoughts about the business. The only rule was that there were no bad ideas. After years of being told ideas were bad by his boss, Tony went the opposite route.

Today, the thriving business is a family affair. Tony is still involved, but Marie and the kids run the 18-store chain (the first four are company-owned; the others are owned and operated by franchisees). Their success is a lesson in the importance of passion, the power of positive thinking, and, most of all, their belief that ideas are the most important part of their success.

THE FIRST YEAR

When they took over that first restaurant, it seemed as though anything was possible, and Tony went wild with his ideas. After years of not being able to get anyone to listen to his insights, Tony was now able to do what he wanted, because he was the boss and doing almost everything by himself. He could just run with an idea—and they worked. In the first six months, the DelVecchios did more in sales than the previous owner did in her best year. Tony says it was more than ideas that made the difference. It was a new mindset he instilled in every employee: Even though something was done a certain way in the past, they should begin each day asking themselves for every task they do, "Is there a better way to do this?" And usually there was. For example:

QGC Pizzas

Tony and Marie were passionate about pizza, and started from scratch every day, hand-tossing the dough and mixing the sauce using his mother's old family recipe that Marie had tweaked. This wasn't anything new, except for the fact that they delivered these gourmet pizzas to your door. That's what made them unique in their area. Even though the couple always intended to create a gourmet pizza delivery service, when they bounced the idea off their daughters (both in college at the time), they confirmed what Tony and Marie already suspected: Young people wanted their pizza cheap, fast, and easy. Great taste was a bonus. But, a more sophisticated, mature, discriminating person would prefer a pizza that wasn't made with pre-packaged ingredients. *That* was their target market, as well as young people who appreciated an authentic pizza pie. When asked, they would tell people, "Our signature pizzas may take a little longer, but they taste much better." Their daughters had a great idea and directed them to create a line of simple pizzas they dubbed QGC Pizzas (quick, good, cheap) for the college crowd.

Contests

Tony would tell anyone who would listen that their pizza (emphasizing the old-world family recipe) was the best in town—and he believed it too. But it was one of his golfing buddies who figured out a way to *prove* it. The foursome would meet at the links on Saturday mornings for what they called the "nine and dine." They'd play nine holes of golf and then head over to the shop for lunch. In the past, while they were playing golf Tony would do most of the talking; many times about his ideas. That's just the way he was. But now that he was running a restaurant, he did a lot less talking and a lot more listening. As an idea guy, Tony could recognize a good idea when he heard one. During the dining part of one particular golf day, his friend said in an offhand way between bites of pizza that Tony and Marie should enter their pizza in a contest, because it was the best in town. Tony took note, and that first year they won an award for having the best pizza in town—the first of two dozen such awards, including one on a national cable-TV food channel.

A Positive View

The recipe for their signature pizzas had been passed down from generation to generation, starting in Italy, and people appreciated the authenticity and great taste. It was the customers' love of everything Italian that gave Marie an idea. The year they took over, three different gangster movies had come out: *Godfather III*, *Goodfellas*, and *Miller's Crossing*. It was also the year John Gotti was arrested for racketeering. A lot of local Italians were worried the portrayal of these mobsters would give others the wrong impression. So Marie invited the local Italian-Americans she knew to come over and discuss ways they could change the perceptions of people in their community. It wasn't a big deal, but the brainstorming gave them something to rally around. They decided to make it their mission to give people a positive Italian experience in their restaurant and beyond. At the second meeting with their fraternity of Italian friends and customers, they came up with some ideas and *ideals* on which to build the business. Marie wanted to pay tribute to Tony's mom, and her parents too, so large photos of each graced the walls alongside some of the most famous Italians of all time. The men's room had famous Italian-American athletes, whereas the ladies room featured female celebrities of Italian descent. The pizza boxes also featured famous Italians and included interesting and inspiring quotations and facts about them. In addition, they set up a small market within the restaurant to sell hard-to-get foods from Italy, and magazines and newspapers from Milan. They taught customers some key words in Italian with translations in their menus. And when the Gulf War started in 1991 they made sure everyone knew Italy had dedicated more than 1,000 troops.

Professional Advice

Being brand new to the restaurant business, the first thing Tony did when he was handed the keys was consult with an expert in addition to the retiring owner. He asked for and received a SCORE counselor (Service Core of Retired Executives), who instantly gave great advice. It was well worth the price—free. For example, his SCORE counselor suggested putting in an old-fashioned suggestion box and getting people to share their notes for improvement. The restaurant even provided crayons and blank paper so people could draw ideas, and Marie created a carnival wheel to spin for a chance to win a free meal if you put a suggestion in the box. Although the idea was old-fashioned, it generated much participation and resulted in numerous excellent ideas, both big and small.

SECOND STORE

With one store under their belt and business booming, it was time to expand, and the Wild Idea Club concept was an integral part of the plan. The DelVecchios were working harder than they ever had, and loving every minute of it. The best part of being their own bosses was the ability to immediately put an idea into action without sending it to "death by committee." By starting from scratch with their second location, they were able to really go wild with their ideas. Here are a few that worked well:

The Italian Experience

Tony wanted to take the Italian experience one step further than it had been done before. During one particularly fruitful Wild Idea Club session, their daughter Anna said, "It's too bad we can't take everyone to Italy to see how close our restaurant is to a real Italian place." In their original restaurant they showed movies on a big-screen TV that Tony had installed along with a VHS player. (Big-screen TVs were unusual at the time, and his generated a lot of word of mouth.) Local sports teams from the community would also come in and watch tapes of themselves playing as they celebrated a win. This one big TV was a big hit. So, what if he had a lot of little televisions, and they showed a continuous loop of some of the famous places in Italy? That's exactly what they did. Tony and Marie had an elaborate mural of the famous Roman Coliseum painted on one of the walls by a local community college art student, and faux windows installed with televisions in each one showing scenes from

Italy on a continuous loop. It made the diners feel as though they were there dining along the canals of Venice or among the hills of Tuscany. They also built in a large fireplace and dedicated space to create three Italian-themed private rooms.

A Little Romance

Around the time the second store opened, a lot of large chain pizza places were taking pizza delivery to the next level, so of course Tony wanted to outdo them—and he did. One of his delivery guys had a great idea: What if they delivered everything a couple would need to have a romantic dinner for two? Or make it a memorable one for the entire family? At the next Wild Idea Club this concept took on a life of its own. For a few extra bucks, delivery orders came with everything needed to have a nice "night out" at home. They delivered checkered tablecloths, wine, candles, and more. The service evolved as customers sent back the suggestion forms that came with each order. One was from a young man who wanted a four-course meal delivered next to the local lake where he was to propose marriage to the girl he'd met there the year before. Tony's employees set up a table and chairs and dressed up for the occasion as they acted as the valet, maitré di, servers, and even sang for the couple. The young woman said "yes."

The Big T

Tony was a big man. He had a large mustache, booming voice, and loud laugh to match. To him, it seemed silly to stuff a pizza as big as his in a tiny box. So he looked for and found giant boxes and used them for deliveries. He also created an enormous 36-inch pizza to fit in this new box. People marveled at the size, and word spread about the "Big T" pizza. It made quite an impression when delivered. Tony also served the Big T to patrons at his place. If two people could finish the entire pizza without any help (no single person could), it was free, and their picture was put on the Big T Wall of Fame. Two firemen earned extra honors for being the first to accomplish the feat.

Doing Good in the Community

For Tony, his business did more than make and sell pizza; he and his wife were an integral part of the community, and it was the pizza that made it possible. So he used the power of pizza for the greater good. He offered students a free slice for every "A" on their report card. He took pizza to striking workers on the picket line. He hosted a guest chef once a week, so that other Italians could create and share their favorite dishes, and the money raised went to their favorite charities. Tony sponsored as many local sports teams as possible, and donated to a number of worthy causes. When a local musician who loved his pizza wanted to do an album launch party at the store, Tony stayed open late and let him play. And he gained plenty of publicity (though his thoughts were purely charitable) one summer night when a student-ministry tour bus broke down in town and Tony let the 14 kids and two adults sleep the night on the floor of his restaurant. Every summer since, when that ministry does its summer tour, they include a lunch stop at the restaurant.

Free Advertising

Someone once told Tony his best marketing tool was the pizza itself—if people could try a piece, they would be hooked. So Tony made it a point to give away as much pizza as possible, and get the most bang for his buck. When a local radio talk-show team did a segment on the things they would want if stranded on a deserted island and mentioned Tony's pizza, he rushed down there with enough pizza for the hosts and crew.

This became a regular ritual until the talk show was moved to the morning-drive time slot. So Tony invented a bacon-and-eggs breakfast pizza and brought that in. (This pizza was a favorite at his restaurants on Sunday mornings and eventually expanded into five types of breakfast pizza.)

An Appetizer Innovation

Tony and Marie had been so fixated on their signature pizzas that they overlooked an item on their menu that was equally as good, if not better, and that was their delicious breadsticks. They were served soft and warm and the aroma made people's mouths water. Before the big pizza chains were doing it, they offered dipping sauces with their breadsticks, and many made that their meal. One day when the wait to get into the restaurant was even longer than usual, one of the hostesses called a quick Wild Idea Club meeting and suggested passing out breadsticks to the hungry patrons waiting in line. This was a big hit and became standard practice whenever there was a significant wait.

TIMES CHANGE; CHANGE WITH THEM

If there was one thing Tony had learned from watching the failing of his former employer and the loss of his job, it was that you not only had to see change coming, but you also had to stay one step ahead of it—and not fear it. So Tony had many firsts in his stores—both in his industry and in his area.

Tony was old school; he personally greeted everyone when possible, and many by name. But he was also savvy enough to be "new school." When his customers' tastes started to change, he was quick to act. In Italy, having an espresso drink after dinner was nothing new, but to be able to get a good one at a *pizza* place was unique. Many of his regulars came in just for the coffee. Tony had always sold pizza by the slice, but there were only a few choices (cheese, pepperoni, and combo). So, many customers wanted mini versions of the larger pizzas for lunch. Tony added them to the menu, and they were an instant hit. Then, when beer trends shifted from Budweiser to micro-brews, Tony and Marie were one of the first places to brew their own line of (award-winning) beers. When health-conscious consumers wanted to eat right (and light), Tony offered to deliver salads with meals. His delivery-order totals rose with the added items that started with salads and went on to include many other items on the menu—several created for calorie counters. And when times got tough for customers, Tony was the first to offer coupons on his best pizzas, and he created "home style" pizzas and pasta dishes that were less expensive for struggling families. He even offered freshly prepared, unbaked pizzas at a discount that could be taken home and cooked (though not the Big T, as it wouldn't fit in anyone's home oven).

BUILDING THE BRAND/GETTING BIGGER

It was bound to happen. When things are going as well as they were for Tony and Marie, others will want to share in the success—and they did. The first person to approach them about expanding the two-store chain through franchising (which was all the rage at the time) was a customer who was moving to a nearby city. The next was one of their original employees ready to start and run a restaurant of his own. By now, Tony's ideas were bigger than just two stores and he was happy to expand. Fortunately, his daughters had done a superb job of branding the business and standardizing. What sealed the deal came when a member of one of Tony's Wild Idea Clubs (formed with the owners of other local businesses) franchised his chain of stores. Quickly, the little pizza place he started a few years earlier was growing into a very big business, and Tony and Marie were thrilled. This allowed him more time to do what he did best—come up with new ideas—and allowed them more time to relax. Franchising also gave him access to even more ideas, some of which became a big part of the franchise's long-term success.

GREAT IDEAS THAT WEREN'T HIS

Now that Tony was "The Boss," he made every effort to encourage creative thinking in his employees—something he would have loved when he wasn't in charge. Now that the company had franchisees, the Wild Idea Club concept was producing new ideas at a rapid rate, and many were a hit. The new owners suggested everything from offering a free pizza to people who came in to celebrate their birthdays to combing the papers for announcements and sending a letter to anyone who was newly promoted to come in for a free lunch. Both of these ideas worked. So did soliciting the minor league baseball team to sell their pizza in the stadium and making the restaurants *the* place to watch sports, with game-day specials and big-screen TVs. Some ideas that seemed not to work at first later turned into successes with further brainstorming. For example, when they switched to new plates featuring famous Italians, the plates would mysteriously disappear. The solution was simple: they made the name of the restaurant more prominent on the plate and added contact information, so if they were "borrowed," at least it could lead to more business. When one of the delivery drivers started his own band on the side he offered to sing when he delivered a pizza—especially if it was a birthday. This was a modest success, but it did make it in the local paper ("Pizza delivered for a song," the headline read) and generated a lot of publicity for the delivery driver.

Other suggestions made by employees included having open kitchens so patrons could see their pizzas being cooked, and this expanded into a once-a-month pizza-making demonstration (in addition to the "guest Italian chef" night). Holding community brainstorming meetings became the norm, with local grocers, hoteliers, travel agents, nutritionists, local leaders, business owners, moms, teens, and customers all participating and contributing suggestions. It was from these people's ideas in the community that Tony and Marie innovated many services in their area: fax ordering (and later, online ordering) for time-crunched workers, curbside delivery for busy parents, a drive-thru pizza window at one location near a highway interchange, and healthier low-fat (and later, low-carb) pizzas. And franchisees weren't ignored either; their input helped improve the concept with each new store, whether it was the business plans, training, supplies, improvements, systems, materials, or management.

There were clearly no limits for Tony and Marie. When managing and running their stores became as smooth as any business could hope for, they went back to the branding blackboard to capitalize on their success. Having learned about the benefits of intellectual property—something that could be created and sold with as much profit (and more) as real estate—they took stock of what they had created: knowledge, an award-winning recipe, business systems, and more. After working with a business consultant for a few months, they took the first step in monetizing their intellectual property by licensing their sauce recipe to a national company. This company, being part of a conglomerate, then connected them with a partner company that made frozen pizzas sold in every major grocery chain in the United States. Next thing you know, Tony and Marie's smiling faces could be seen behind the frosty glass of the freezer at your local store. And it was this very thing that led to what they called "the book."

Neither Tony nor Marie had ever thought of themselves as potential authors. But as a result of an acquisitions editor at a major book publisher seeing their frozen pizzas in a store, buying one, enjoying it, and then reading Tony and Marie's philosophy blurb on the back of the box, they found themselves in bookstores as well. The book, *Life Lessons From Pizza*, was a glossy hardcover combination of philosophy, business advice, recipes, relationship guidance, memoir, and a dash of spirituality that caught the book world by surprise (not to mention Tony and Marie). Next thing she knew, Marie was seeing her name on the various bestseller lists, right there next to some of her favorite authors. And for the two of them, that summer became one they'll never forget—doing a national book tour in an RV that opened on the side for pizza-making demonstrations wherever they stopped. When one local reporter asked Tony what he saw as the biggest life lesson from pizza, he didn't hesitate to say, "You can truly make it anything you want."

Chapter Four
Organizing the Chaos

Mind Mapping...because ideas don't travel in straight lines...
—Chic Thompson

It was 5 a.m. as Shawn pulled into the gated complex to pick up Patty. Since meeting in yoga class eight years earlier, they'd remained close friends, and he often filled in as her "airport chauffeur."

Shawn lifted her two heavy bags into his truck. "You need *all* this for a three-day trip?"

Patty sleepily replied, "An entire suitcase is filled with my markers and supplies." He shook his head and handed her the 27-page client report he had printed out because her printer was on the fritz. Report in hand, Patty shuffled to the passenger door and let herself in.

Not quite two hours later, Patty was getting comfortable aboard the plane, starting to come to life and counting her blessings that no one was in the middle seat. As the 737 climbed through the clouds and the sun cracked the horizon, she wistfully gazed out the window. *How fun*, she thought, *I'm returning to Milwaukee. If we finish the project early, maybe I can swing by the Harley-Davidson company store and buy some new gear.*

Her smile quickly vanished as she recalled the last time she was sent on assignment to Stratford Confectioners' corporate headquarters. Talk about chaos...

"No, no, no. That idea will never work!" shouted one amazingly negative guy with a comb-over pasted to the top of his head.

"We talked about that last month," grumbled a woman, thoroughly engrossed in her French manicure.

"This project should be further along by now," said another middle-management mook.

And then, of course, there were the perennial favorites:

"We tried that already."

"We don't have the budget for that."

But the best came from a caffeine-crazed guy named Carl who silenced the room with, "You're a bunch of egomaniacs with your brains up your butts!"

Apparently not noticing the room had in fact shut up, Senior VP of Marketing William Saunders put his foot down with a loud "SHUT UP!" Realizing with embarrassment that his voice had probably carried quite a ways down the hall, his face turned bright pink. The few wispy hairs left on his scalp slowly danced in the breeze from the air-conditioning vent overhead. This group had routinely tested his British reserve, but today was exceptional. Perhaps it was his own stress, however, making things worse in his mind—Stratford Confectioners was the oldest and most reputable chocolate manufacturer in the United Kingdom, and he had the daunting task of launching their brand in the $13-billion U.S. market.

💡 💡 💡

William was tired of wasting his company's resources; their meetings had become such a waste of time and money. Worse yet, his people were showing the wear of stress as well: Every day they looked more defeated, creativity was lacking, and sales were down.

Shortly after that chaotic and unproductive sales meeting, William traveled to Boston on Southwest Airlines. He sighed and thought, *They are one of the most innovative companies in the United States—they incorporate their employees' ideas and it impacts the airline's bottom line. Besides that, it looks like their employees enjoy their work and have fun, unlike my crew.*

How could he change the dynamics of his team? William wanted them *all* to be happy, and if he didn't turn things around soon, his job was in jeopardy. With a new house and three kids in college, he couldn't afford for that to happen.

There was no hiding his frustration, but as he continued flipping through the in-flight magazine his headache began to fade, and soon he was laughing so hard he almost choked on a peanut.

"What's so funny?" asked the guy in the aisle seat.

"I'm reading about this Italian guy named Tony who started a fledgling gourmet pizza business 20 years ago and now he's really successful."

"And what's so funny about that?"

"Well, he started this thing called a Wild Idea Club with his employees, and you should hear some of their ideas. Plus, you wouldn't believe what this guy is worth! Stumbling onto this article just made my day. You have no idea." He passed the magazine over to the guy, open to the article on Tony.

Later, on the ground at Logan Airport, he practically tripped over the gate agent as he departed—he couldn't wait to activate his BlackBerry and find out more about this Wild Idea Club concept.

Could this be the solution he was looking for?

It was right after this that Patty had gotten the call from William that put her on the early-morning flight to Wisconsin.

"Are you available on Wednesday?" William eagerly asked her, as his limo navigated its way through Beantown. "Great! I'm sending the entire brand team for an emergency session— and bring all of your stuff!" He was suddenly feeling energized. This meeting was going to be a success.

He was so grateful he had discovered Patty's talent at an annual conference for marketing professionals. Sitting next to her, he couldn't help being distracted by the drawings she was doing during the presentations. He had to know more. Afterward they met over a martini and Patty summed it up: "I facilitate all of my meetings incorporating graphic expression. It's such a powerful tool to capture your best ideas and keep the group on track." It wasn't long after that meeting that William invited Patty to the corporate offices in Wisconsin just to observe his team in action. He was embarrassed at the way his staff had behaved, especially with an outside consultant.

As William checked into the Cambridge Hyatt Regency he thought, *The outcome of this meeting is going to be different—I can feel it.* He decided he was going to allow Patty and her partner to run the meeting, and use it as a chance to incorporate all he could learn about the Wild Idea Club. Beaming and more relaxed, he'd actually just implemented one of the club suggestions he'd learned in the in-flight magazine article: Invite others from outside your organization to participate.

💡 💡 💡

Patty loved her job and she loved working with Stacie. Stacie was one of those consummate creatives—a perfect blend of business acumen and off-the-wall creativity. She was organic in appearance, yet brilliantly savvy as a facilitator. She had to be, working with senior level VPs, researchers, and scientists who were proven experts in their fields, as well as highly innovative brand strategists, creative marketers, and advertising types.

Stacie and Patty had met several years ago in Monterey, California, at the annual conference for visual practitioners. Patty had been amazed to find out there was a community of visual communicators working in that field for more than 25 years. The retreat facility was small, but big enough to accommodate the group of 50. Each breakout room had been temporarily wallpapered with white butcher paper. This group wasn't your typical batch of conference attendees—everyone was equipped with sketch pads and markers, as well as Birkenstocks and fleecy Patagonia vests. They were down to earth, authentic, and creative in spite of being brilliant and accomplished.

Dr. Suresh Patel, a neuroscientist from Stanford, and Wilhelmina Smith, an MFA from Berkeley, were the presenters. Their workshops centered on the functioning of the brain and the power of integrating visual language as part of the problem-solving and learning process. The teachings were powerful and provocative.

On the first day, Patty and Stacie were paired up on an activity demonstrating how to best capture, record, and follow through on solutions generated at meetings. Stacie was the gifted facilitator working in tandem with Patty, who served as the graphic recorder or strategic illustrator. Her job was to draw everyone's ideas as they were sharing them. Similar to a live translator hearing Spanish and speaking English in real time, Patty's role demanded listening to everything being said and making quick interpretations. She was known for her exuberance with clients: "I transform the concepts and ideas into visual icons and images. It's the coolest thing!"

Patty and Stacie had a great time the entire weekend, and throughout the years their friendship had grown into a successful consulting practice dedicated to teaching others how to use the various tools and methods they had learned at that conference. Their clients came from a multitude of industries, including auto manufacturing, technology, healthcare, property management, credit services, consumer goods, retail, hospitality, and restaurants.

Now, they had added the Stratford Confectioners account to their list—a bonus, as both were self-proclaimed "chocaholics" and always came home with complimentary samples.

💡 💡 💡

William arrived in Milwaukee early Tuesday afternoon and called to see if Patty's and Stacie's flights had arrived on time. He was eager to get everything prepped for the next day's ideation-brainstorming session. "I have arranged for us to meet off site in a funky art gallery that showcases local talent," he told them. "It has a hip vibe yet a relaxed, comfortable feel. It will beat meeting in our stuffy conference room." It wasn't long afterward that "Team Patty and Stacie" arrived at Lunchbox Studios, across the street from their boutique hotel. William proudly led them inside.

"Oh, this is so cool, I *love* it!" Patty said as she entered, her eyes wide with excitement. "Look at the floor-to-ceiling windows—

great light, and I love the empty wall space we can use to post our 'gallery of ideas.'"

"These moving dividers will help us stay focused and keep the concepts separated," Stacie added. "And the artwork..." She paused, not having to say another word, knowing Patty understood how much the provocative pieces would help stimulate creative thoughts and ideas. Stacie moved closer to study a painting of a woman standing on a upward-pointing pencil.

"William, you picked an excellent venue!" said Patty. "Your team is going to see a different side of your management style. You'll score big points. Did you have time to buy the prizes?"

"Yes, I did. I found some great bottles of vintage cabs and merlots that will also work well for our chocolate-and-wine-pairing exercise."

Patty began to unpack her small attaché of professional markers while Stacie was talking to Cody, the onsite coordinator, to see if all of the supplies had arrived. "Good news: they arrived this morning," he reported. "We also have the easels and tables you requested. Celebrity Balloons will be here first thing in the morning with your order."

"Great," she said. "I need to put together the check-in bags before the team arrives. You guys can finish setting up the room." She headed back across the street to the hotel.

William was impressed. "Patty, I am learning a lot from you. I'd have never thought to set up a room like this—sorting out all these details is certainly worth the time and expense. We're setting the stage for a phenomenal meeting."

"Great, I am glad you feel that way," she said. "We still have a lot of work to do, so could you unpack those flip-chart pads and put them on all the easels?" She pointed to the large box that Cody had brought out from the back room. "Make sure each round table has a flip-chart stand next to it, and we'll need three more stands set up over in that corner for my work."

Right after that, William also unpacked the big photo boards he had shipped in from the art department. "Look, Patty, I had our graphics department enlarge these photos of people enjoying our products. I love the one of the two-year-old with his face covered in chocolate—that's actually Henry's youngest son."

"When will Henry be here?" Patty asked. Henry Richardson was the brand manager who would be kicking off the next day's meeting with an overview of Stratford's brand strategies for the United States. "I almost forgot we'll need to set up a table and extension cord for his computer. We can project his presentation on the butcher-paper wall that we'll use later as our idea gallery."

"What else do we need to do?" asked William.

She never looked up from her search for an extension cord as she answered him. "Check the supply boxes on all the tables, please. They should have scissors, markers, Post-it notes, index cards, glue sticks, and pens inside." Then she remembered the magazines and looked up to see if they'd arrived. "See the stack of magazines? Make sure you mix them up and put several of each on all the tables."

William wasn't familiar with some of the magazines—*Real Simple, Bon Appetit, Wine Spectator, Cigar Aficionado, Body and Soul*—but some he'd seen many times—*Martha Stewart Living, Oprah, Gourmet, Travel, Food & Wine, Vogue*, and of course, *Chocolate Magazine*.

Patty was just finishing setting out all of her supplies when Stacie returned. "Oh my God," she said. "This is one of the best setups I've ever seen. You guys outdid yourselves—this environment looks amazing!"

Patty asked her, "Did you bring your iPod? William and I forgot ours. We need to get some upbeat music playing ASAP to fight off the jet lag."

Stacie rarely went anywhere without her iPod. "How about some Rolling Stones?" she asked, remembering Patty had said he was a big fan. Moments later, "Paint It Black" was rocking from her small, portable but amazing-sounding speakers.

Stacie's focus was immediately drawn to the product table that was now set up. Working on a chocolate brand was far more fun than brainstorming about air conditioning units. William's executive assistant had done an excellent job of finding multiple varieties to work with.

"Look at this," Stacie said, looking as if she might literally drool. "There are ones with almonds, cashews, pistachios, fruits—raspberry, orange, raisins—truffles, solid bars, and some sugar-free ones. Awesome!" William's assistant had also sent packaging forms for hot cocoa, popcorn, sauces...even liquid soap. "These will really stimulate creative thought," Stacie said.

Even with the Stones' energy in the room, it was only a little while later that Stacie noticed Patty and William starting to drag. She knew Patty often worried about things the night before these events and probably hadn't slept well, not to mention the predawn trip to the airport. Stacie, on the other hand, was getting a late-afternoon burst of energy. "Why don't the two of you freshen up for dinner," she said, "and I'll take care of the remaining details with Cody."

💡 💡 💡

Back across the street at the Knickerbocker Hotel, the Stratford team was starting to arrive, and the first to check in was Ji-Young Park. She was the newest member of the marketing group, a recent MBA graduate from Wharton, and the first

Korean woman to work for the company. Ji-Young looked surprised when the front desk clerk handed her a brightly colored gift bag. "What's this?" she asked. The clerk smiled, having been clued in by William earlier in the afternoon.

"It's from Mr. Saunders, and he instructed us to have you open it when you get to your room."

Once there, she couldn't wait, and as soon as she dropped her laptop bag on the bed Ji-Young pulled out a brown box with a purple ribbon wrapped around it. She discovered one of Stratford's premium chocolates with a note attached:

Welcome to Stratford Confectioner's first Wild Idea Club session! This is your homework assignment:
(1) Save your chocolate until after the
hotel's turndown service.
(2) At that time, slowly and deliberately eat the hotel's chocolate, then our chocolate, and answer the following questions about both brands: Describe the texture; how does it feel as it melts on your tongue?
Does it have an aroma? What is the color and shape?
Tell us about the packaging. Any other observations?
Please bring your paper with you tomorrow morning.
This exercise will start our brainstorming process.
We are excited to have you join us!
Gratefully, Henry and William

Ji-Young smiled. *This is going to be fun!*

The art gallery was getting ready to lock up for the night. Signs were posted saying that it will be closed to the public on Wednesday for a special Wild Idea Club meeting. Stacie had stressed to Cody how important confidentiality was—all of the ideas and activities being proprietary. They even had a code name for the meeting: The Wonka Project.

Stacie took one last glance around the room. "Patty is an amazing artist," she said to Cody.

He agreed. "What a great idea to create a welcome poster with everyone's name on it," he said.

Stacie went over to the facilitator's table to make sure everything was in check: activity sheets, timer, agenda, fabric, tissue paper. The digital video camera was tucked underneath the table, and she pulled it out to show Cody. "We use this to capture the day and all the great ideas without slowing things down."

♀ ♀ ♀

Later, as Patty, Stacie, William, and Henry all sat in the hotel restaurant finishing off their desserts, they had moved past the personal and social talk and started to think about the next day.

"What time are we meeting in the morning?" asked Henry.

"We should plan to have breakfast over at the gallery so we can go over any last-minute details," answered William. "Patty, do you think 7 a.m. will give us enough time?"

"That should work," she said, between bites of her tiramisu.

Stacie needed to go over the participant list in order to thoughtfully put together the work teams. "Is everyone coming from R&D?"

Henry replied: "Natraj Guresh, Trevor Halliday, Antwon Jones, and Hong Chu, plus five more are confirmed. Trudy Gardner might be stuck in Minneapolis, though. Big storm. But fortunately, it's not supposed to hit here until after we're all on our planes tomorrow. Fingers crossed."

"What about marketing?" Stacie followed up.

"That'll be Ji-Young Park, Suzy Roberts, John Taylor, Brooke Pennington, and four others," answered William. "We also have people coming from the PR and advert agencies—that'll add eight more."

"Excellent!" Stacie said as she noted the names on her pad. Patty smiled at Stacie's endless exuberance.

The following morning, long before the alarm was due to go off, Patty was awake at 4 a.m. She couldn't help it. She always got antsy on these big days, but the extra time never hurt—she could do her yoga stretches and take a quick run to calm her nerves. It wasn't a bad nervous, but like a professional comedian, athlete, or other performer, it was inevitable to be anxious. After all, she *was* a performer, drawing in front of crowds that sometimes numbered in the hundreds.

She stood at the window, overlooking the darkened meeting venue a few floors below on the opposite side of the street. There wasn't yet even a hint of sunlight, and the world outside had the same stillness as the one she had stepped outside to nearly 24 hours earlier at home. To her left, down the block, a solitary traffic light ran dutifully through its green-yellow-red cycle, oblivious to the lack of cars. She finished off her cup of hot tea, then turned from the window to roll out her yoga mat.

When the four of them arrived at Lunchbox Studios a few hours later, the space looked impressive. There were clusters of balloons everywhere and the caterers had done a fabulous job laying out healthy food choices: lox, bagels, fresh fruit, eggs, granola, turkey bacon, and homemade carrot bran muffins. They even had an espresso machine and barista ready to take orders.

"I'll take a cappuccino," requested Patty, and while it was being made, she started drawing the flip-chart templates that would help the groups capture all their ideas.

It was about 8 o'clock when the team started rolling in, and everyone could feel the energy and excitement in the room. It was especially fun for William to observe them as he thought to himself, *They don't look as stressed out as they typically do. I can't wait for this to start.*

At 8:30 he gathered his team from the breakfast bar and instructed them to take a seat at any of the tables. "Welcome to our very first Wild Idea Club brainstorming session for Stratford Confectioners. I am excited to have with us two special ladies who travel all over the world helping companies like ours learn how to capture their best ideas and follow through with them. Meet Patty Lawson from Southern California and Stacie Ewing from Denver, Colorado." Everyone enthusiastically applauded as Patty and Stacie nodded in acknowledgment.

"You were all hand-picked to participate in this unique session," William continued. "The company has invested a lot of resources to bring you here. It's important that you are on time and engaged in everything we do; therefore I ask that you turn off your PDAs. This is one day when we can focus on nothing but ideas and chocolate." In the background, the espresso machine made a swooshing sound as someone's latté was being made.

"Besides that, the only other rule is: there are no bad ideas!" He then gestured to Henry, who was standing behind him. "Now I'd like to bring up Henry Richardson, who will give us a brand overview on the U.S. market."

Henry proceeded with his PowerPoint presentation of data and bullet points and the outcomes the group needed to achieve by the end of the day. But more than simply a factual presentation, it was intended to lay the groundwork for encouraging the group to believe they could achieve a lot during the day. And so, the presentation included carefully selected motivational quotations, inspiring images, and examples of what "success" would mean for the meeting. As he turned off the projector, Henry turned the meeting over to Stacie and Patty.

Patty was already standing at the wall where the welcome poster was hanging and had a marker in hand. Stacie said, "We're going to jump right in. Introduce yourselves and tell everyone what aspect of the business you're in, and then tell us what your favorite dessert is. I'll start. I'm your facilitator for today's meeting and I absolutely love Ben & Jerry's Chunky Monkey ice cream." Patty simultaneously started drawing a banana and monkey next to Stacie's name, and she could hear a few people mutter, "Cool." The intros continued and the poster was soon filling up with images of cookies, pies, sundaes, cheesecake, custard, and one soufflé. The group continued having fun testing Patty's skills as they called out some bizarre choices, including "apricot-rhubarb-pecan pie with chocolate sauce," to which Patty gave the person a playful look of disbelief before rendering an impressive illustration of the request. Everyone nodded in approval as William smiled, seeing Patty had won them over.

It was a fun way to start the day. The group started letting down their guard and had the best laugh of the intros when Hong Chu said he liked Peking Dust (fresh-ground chestnuts with whipped cream) and Patty started drawing Peking Duck.

After the intros and laughter had died down, Patty went over to the flip-chart stands she had put side-by-side. Earlier she had prepped a number of pages in anticipation of capturing the team's responses to the homework questions. The yellow-bordered charts would serve to group the comments about the hotel's chocolate, and the purple-bordered ones were for Stratford's.

Stacie went over to one of the yellow charts to demonstrate an idea-capturing process called mind-mapping. She had Patty draw an oval in the middle of the paper and write the word *taste* in the center. She turned to the group and asked, "How did the hotel chocolate taste last night?"

"It tasted like it expired five years ago," someone shouted from the back. Patty drew a line coming out of the center to another drawn oval with the word *old* in it. Someone else said "like cardboard," so she drew another line (like a branch) coming out of the *taste* oval and connected it to a drawn piece of cardboard. As the group called out their answers, Patty worked fast and furiously to record what they were saying both in words and images. Sometimes there was an overlap—when someone else said "like paper" Patty drew a line from the cardboard oval and wrote "paper" in another oval to show the connection between similar items.

Once they had filled seven sheets for the hotel, they repeated the process for their own brand (with unsurprisingly better comments). Soon, the walls were covered with more than a dozen sheets of funny-looking mind-maps filled with words and images.

"Wow," Stacie said, pulling the group's attention back from the sheets to her. "We got all that done and it's only 9:15— we're right on time." Part of Stacie's job was to keep them on track, allowing William and Henry to participate like all the others. She knew that it's good to put boundaries even on a creative process.

For the next exercise, she intentionally mixed up everyone's places at the tables. Each included two R&D folks, two marketing people, and one agency rep. She and Patty would circulate to assist if the groups got stuck.

One woman started opening the box in the middle of the table. "Look at all of these cool supplies," she said. The guy next to her was already paging through the *Cigar Aficionado* magazine.

Stacie called everyone to attention and gave the instructions for their next task. "You have all been given some magazines that represent what our target market is reading. Come up with a group name for yourselves, then write it as the title, like a headline, on your flip-chart pad. Then sort through the magazines and cut out any words or images that fit your perception of Stratford's brand. There is a glue stick in your box—make a collage to present to the group, and feel free to draw or add words if you can't find them in the magazine." Stacie went over to the iPod docking station and turned on The Who. Patty appreciated her knowledge of classic rock, even though Stacie liked '80s music more. It had made for some funny conversations years ago when Patty talked about "real" classic rock, given that most classic-rock stations were starting to play songs from the 1980s and even early 1990s.

Patty and Stacie worked around the room for the next half-hour or more, helping everyone with their projects, eventually determining when the group had reached a productive stopping point.

"Okay, who's ready to present their collage?" called out Stacie. The group that went first had named themselves "The Turtles"—chosen because they all liked that type of chocolate and the band by the same name. One by one each group presented their ideas, after which William complimented the entire bunch. "I can't believe there aren't any similarities," he said. "Each one is uniquely amazing and captures the collective creativity of the group. An impressive lot." Privately, he was astounded that many of these same people couldn't have been counted on to act civil in many past meetings.

Stacie announced to the group that they had earned a 15-minute break. At first no one got up, as they were still chatting with each other. You would have thought they had been friends for years. But eventually most everyone took to more of the fabulous food and got a second (or third) coffee drink.

Patty remembered seeing most of this group on her very first visit to Stratford. During the break she commented to William, "I can hardly believe this is the same group of people. Look at them—their faces are animated, the laughter is contagious, and you can feel the excitement in the room."

William was practically in tears. "I know. I'm so grateful I stumbled onto this concept. I was beginning to think I needed to pull out the ol' C.V.—resumé, as you call it here in the States."

When they returned from the break, there were names on each of the boards—the groups had changed. Each table now had a mountain of fabric, pipe cleaners, paints, sequins, glitter, ribbon, tags, beads, and more.

"Oh no," cried out Natraj, chief engineer in R&D, "I hate crafts!" *This is gonna be good*, Stacie thought. *There are five guys in that group.*

Stacie proceeded to tell everyone they needed to construct packaging ideas for Stratford chocolates. They could work together and create as many as possible in 30 minutes.

"30 minutes?" groaned Trudy, who had decided to drive from Minneapolis to beat the big storm. "That's not enough time."

"See what you can do," Stacie responded as she pressed play on the iPod. To change things up, this time it wasn't classic rock but classical—Prokofiev.

The next hour was filled with laughter and applause as they constructed and presented their ideas, proudly displaying them on the tables near the windows until it was time to give out the first prize.

William reached under the facilitator's table and said, "I'd like to award this handsome bottle of 1998 Reserve Robert Mondavi Cabernet Sauvignon to Antwon"—the group let out a huge round of applause as he blushed—"for stretching outside his comfort zone and creating what could be a very innovative and marketable idea." The applause continued as Antwon took the bottle from William, who said to Stacie, "Make sure we follow through and send the prototype to the design team in Dallas, please."

It wasn't long before each group became very proud of their ideas. Outbursts of "Barricade the entrance!" became the running joke as each group thought they had the next million-dollar idea and knew it would be top-secret industry news.

By this point, everyone eagerly awaited their next assignment almost like preschool kids. This one would be done solo and take them outdoors—being in nature lends itself to creative thought and the fresh air would revitalize those who had just flown in from Europe. Fortunately, the street for three blocks in either direction from the studio was lined with benches, and there was a park around the corner.

This away activity also gave Patty and Cody time to prep for the surprise lunch. Lunchbox Studios had a garden café that was hidden from the street view. Guest pastry chef Tobi Sherman of Sherman Desserts & Delicacies was already in the kitchen directing her staff. Cody had made sure the red wine was open by 11:30 to allow time to breathe. Tobi sampled the fondue, then surveyed the filet mignon and roasted vegetables. *Boy, is everyone in for a surprise*, she thought.

Tobi had never imagined her work would involve partnering with consumer food companies. She was old-school and whipped up whatever she felt like—no matter if anyone else liked it or not. Her reputation spread rapidly, and soon everyone on the East Coast made her restaurant a must-stop. She even had one of the most-popular food shows on cable TV.

When everyone came back in from their outside activity, Stacie had them tape all of their letter-sized sheets on the 14-foot blank wall. Ten sheets times 25 people equaled 250 instant ideas. Later, they could sort them out to see if there were any duplicates, but for the time being, the goal was unbridled quantity.

After everyone's idea sheets were on the wall and the group took a quick peek at each other's creations, Stacie led them to the back garden. While they all stood wondering what was next, Stacie brought out and introduced chef Tobi. A few people in the group whispered words of recognition of the TV chef.

"In preparing lunch for you," Tobi started, "I was given the task of pairing foods with Stratford chocolates. I hope these will please your palate." Tobi then went on to explain why she chose each item and how it was incorporated.

As everyone savored all of the delicacies and intricacies of the flavors and aromas throughout the 90 minutes, Henry videotaped their comments to be later edited and distributed on DVD. It would be part memento and part future idea-generation. Best of all, Henry had a personality suited to asking them questions that would generate both hilarious and insightful comments on camera.

Now that the group was seasoned in the Wild Idea Club ways, the afternoon activities became more challenging. They needed to accomplish the outcomes that Henry presented, and so he selected the partners for the next exercise.

"I need everyone to think about which celebrity best represents our brand," he said. "Then create a 30-second commercial that will be acted out for the group. Use a flip-chart to storyboard your spot. And yes, we will be videotaping these!

But don't worry, they won't end up on YouTube." Most everyone laughed, though a few did more nervously at the mere thought.

The next hour was spent developing and watching the 12 commercials. Henry had made sure each pair of people included at least one extrovert, and there were a few hams in the group, which helped. And this was a great exercise to tap into all the "class clowns," to make use of their talents and give them their moment to shine. It worked: Three of the commercials generated uproarious laughter, and one was even a contender for real-commercial status. Maybe Henry shouldn't have excluded YouTube...

"I am totally surprised at how much energy everyone still has," commented Stacie after the commercial session. "Okay, you earned it—take a 15-minute break and meet back here promptly at 3 sharp. There is one more thing we need to do."

Although everyone had plenty to eat during lunch, there was no shortage of people at the snack table, gathering mixed nuts and cheese blocks onto their plates like a mischief of mice. Free and plentiful food was always a welcome thing, as Patty and Stacie had learned long ago. And to keep the group charged, there was an ample selection of energy drinks on a bucket of ice.

"All right," Stacie said after the break. "Look around this room at all your creativity—this *all* came from *you*! Do you believe we did all this in one day?" There was spontaneous applause, and then Stacie encouraged everyone to high-five those around them. "Great job, great job. Okay, now Patty will be giving each of you a strip of 10 dot stickers. Take your time and go around the room looking at *everything*—the packaging ideas, the collage charts, the gallery of ideas, all of it—and put your dots next to anything that excites you. If it really excites you then you may put a couple of dots on the same concept. Got it?"

While everybody was contemplating their choices, Stacie and Patty made sure to collect all of the papers that had been left on the tables; even people's doodles and seemingly insignificant notes could prove to be useful. They then asked William and Henry to arrange the chairs in a circle and place a card and pen on each chair.

After the group sat down in their new circle, Stacie asked them to reflect on the day and think about one thing they wish the Stratford brand would do. Patty was up at the flip-chart again, ready to capture everyone's feedback as a final record of the day. She had drawn a special banner: "These are what I call the golden nuggets of the day—this is when we bring it all home!"

Ji-Young went first. "I wish Stratford would align itself with a cause, like making sure we aren't breaking any child labor laws on the cocoa plantations, and advertise that."

"I hope we include on our packaging that we use certified organic ingredients and no pesticides," added Suzy.

Hong Chu said, "I would like to see acai berries added to the dark chocolate bars." This prompted a few "Mmmms" from around the room.

After all 25 of them shared, William congratulated everyone on their input, adding, "These are all completely viable." He then asked if there were any more observations from the day, and a reticent PhD named John Taylor spoke up.

"After today, I'll admit, I have a much greater respect for the marketing department. All of us in R&D always thought they were a bunch of fluff, but we now see how hard their job is."

John's sincere statement prompted a round of applause from everyone in the room who didn't work in marketing, after which William thanked the entire group for an extraordinary day.

"Look around the room," he said with a wide-sweeping gesture toward all they had done. "This is your work! It may take us some time to implement some of your ideas, but I want to commend you on working collaboratively. I hope that you will share the power of the Wild Idea Club with your colleagues." He then motioned for Patty, Stacie, and Henry to stand near him.

"As far as next steps, the four of us will be meeting tomorrow to look over all of this. We will be taking digital photos of the charts so they can be printed and bound together in a Stratford Wild Idea Club booklet. We'll also be shipping all the charts back to corporate. And Natraj, the word is out—you are creative!" Everyone cheered while Natraj stood and took a dramatic bow.

William continued: "I will also have the IT guys set up an FTP site for you and your colleagues to log in to. We invite you to share what this is all about. And now that the business part is over, I have two more prizes left." He held up a pair of oversized, decorated envelopes. "Let's have a round of applause for our amazing co-facilitators." And not only did everyone applaud, but it was a standing ovation. "For Stacie, I have a $250 spa certificate for the Ritz Carlton, and for Patty, a Harley-Davidson gift card!"

💡 💡 💡

During the next five years, Stratford Confectioner's market share grew by 13 percent, unheard of for a newcomer. They launched the brand in China, Dubai, and India. The CEO was so impressed that she created a new position for William: Director of Global Innovation. And it included a hefty raise plus a vacation home in the Swiss Alps. Stratford offices in all five countries had ongoing Wild Idea Clubs—out of which came their immensely successful fudge-chocolate ice cream bar. William concentrated his efforts on training key staff members in the area of innovation, continuing to seek creative and unique ideas for their brand. And many of the original charts created at Lunchbox Studios still hang on the walls at their corporate offices in Milwaukee. Although William's achievements were written up in many business magazines, his favorite to this day is the one that ultimately appeared in the Southwest Airlines magazine.

Chapter Five
The Perfect Pitch

If you have an apple and I have an apple and we exchange these apples, then you and I will still each have one apple. But if you have an idea and I have an idea and we exchange these ideas, then each of us will have two ideas.
—George Bernard Shaw

Aaron looked out the window from his office as a couple dozen employees from his company filed into a rented bus. They were all headed to a Washington Redskins game on an unusually balmy October evening. It was just past 5:30, and although Aaron would've been more than happy to be on the bus, he was content to watch the beaming workers as they laughed and joked with each other in the parking lot. And the mood wasn't any less festive on the bus, as anyone could clearly see through the windows.

Once the last person climbed aboard, the door closed, and within a minute the bus rambled its way out to the street, turned left, and disappeared behind some trees. Aaron could see a slight smile on his face in his reflection in the window, his skin cast in an orange glow from the soon-setting sun. As he swiveled his chair back around to face his computer, he thought about how much things had changed in the company in the past few years. Although the people were basically the same, the work was the same, and they were in the same building, it almost seemed to be a different company. He moved aside a stack of papers that had grown higher than the little statuette behind them; the small brass plaque at the base of the statuette read:

EXEMPLARY SERVICE AWARD

10-YEAR EMPLOYMENT ANNIVERSARY PRESENTED TO

AARON CAMPBELL

The bonus that came with the award was substantial—$7,500—on top of a $55,000 salary. And it was very unusual in the air-courier industry. Although the company invoiced tons of money, which Aaron oversaw as head of the billing department, there were considerable expenses in getting vital packages and shipments from point A to point B nearly anywhere in the world. Unlike an overnight service such as FedEx, Aaron's company specialized in same-day service; for example, when an airplane sits at a gate waiting for an emergency repair, that airline will pay a considerable fee to get the necessary part to the airport from anywhere. Otherwise, that plane is just an expensive decoration.

Handsome bonuses and trips to see Monday night football weren't always the norm at the company. The philosophy at the company when Aaron started almost 11 years earlier was very different: because profit margins were thin, money wasn't to be handed out frivolously for perks. It wasn't that the industry had changed since then, or even that profitability had changed; it was the management mindset that had changed. But in fact, profitability *had* changed—for the better—once the philosophy shifted to one of openness to employee creativity. What goes around comes around.

The shift was the result of two key events. One was the "moving on" of an obstacle by the name of Norman Greenbaum. Greenbaum had been a fixture at the company for more than 20 years. Everyone suspected he had some dirt on the owner, because despite being one of the most negative people you could meet, he somehow kept his job. He prided himself on turning down everything from vacation requests to purchases of office supplies to promotions. In fact, Norman used to say, without a hint of joking, "My name starts with 'no' for a reason." As the gods would have it, however, he missed Nancy Reagan's memo to "just say no" and found himself arrested for possessing illegal prescription drugs at an airport.

The second key occurrence that helped shift the company's philosophy came from Aaron himself. After Greenbaum's sudden departure, there were the typical personnel changes, which included Aaron's promotion to billing manager. While celebrating with a friend over lunch soon after, he learned about the Wild Idea Club.

"That's what you should put in place there," said Aaron's friend, Tom, as he dipped his chip into the salsa.

"What is it?"

"It's a way for employees at a company to form small groups and come up with ideas. You know, quit complaining and start solving problems." Tom munched a couple more chips while

Aaron thought about it. "Now that you're mister big manager guy, Aaron, you're going to be dealing with a lot more than just making sure your sheet balances on Friday."

In all the excitement about the promotion, Aaron hadn't actually thought much of dealing with employees. But it was true. Thanks to the shake-up after Greenbaum did his drug-smuggler impersonation, Aaron's wasn't just a manager in title—he was going to actually be managing nine employees.

"Okay," he said to Tom. "You got my attention. Tell me all about this Wild Idea Club concept." And Tom proceeded to tell him exactly how a coworker had set it up at his company and what a huge difference it had made.

♀ ♀ ♀

"How was the game?" Aaron asked. It was the morning after and time for the monthly Wild Idea Club meeting. Because the Redskins had won, those in the conference room who cared were in a particularly good mood.

"It was awesome!" replied Sarah, who worked in operations and only recently started with the company straight out of college. Lucas, an African-American man in his 50s with graying hair at his temples, enthusiastically nodded in agreement.

"Excellent," said Aaron. "It's a great stadium to be at. I was pretty stoked just watching on TV." Aaron looked around the room and saw that everyone had arrived. "Gretchen, could you close the door, please? Thanks."

For this particular Wild Idea Club (there were four companywide), it was only their third meeting. And all but three of the people in the room hadn't been a part of the Wild Idea Club concept since it started last year. So, for this meeting, Aaron wanted to focus on how to best pitch ideas.

He divided the group into four teams of three people each, making sure to spread the more experienced "clubbers" each into a separate team. And just to keep it fun and silly, each team was assigned one of four names: The Goobers, The Dinguses, The Doof-wads, and The Boners. Not one to miss an opportunity to exploit the situation, Aaron even came to the meeting prepared with paper hats, each adorned with a team name. The simple act of distributing the hats, with everyone reading their team names, generated a fair amount of laughter—but nothing compared to the oath each person had to speak aloud. Ben McLaren led it off:

"I, Ben McLaren, pledge allegiance to The Boners." He held his right hand up for full effect. "I pledge to fully participate, provide positive feedback, and help generate wild ideas that will benefit the company and each of us." Most likely, few people heard much of what Ben said, as the room roared in laughter.

After the noise died down and the last oath was given, Aaron—still smiling, pleased with his hat coup—led the group into the "serious" part of the meeting. About six months earlier, the company had invested a considerable sum into outfitting the conference room Aaron's Wild Idea Club was meeting in. As he did from time to time, he looked around the room, rediscovering the numerous touches that really helped make these meetings productive.

Instead of the obligatory rectangular, oblong conference-room table, this room boasted a wave-shaped one that would look like a shallow "S" from above. It also sat at one end of the unusually large room, leaving a sizable open area, which allowed for gathering away from the table, sitting on the floor, or standing group sessions—all intended to inspire movement and creativity. In fact, this area was used by a weekly company yoga class. Lastly, everything had been done to ensure that the expression of ideas could flow as easily as possible: roughly 85 percent of the wall space in the room was a magnetic whiteboard surface that could be written or drawn on with dry-erase markers, used to post papers and other printed items, or for whatever clever use anyone could dream up. In the corner sat a decorative cabinet that held colored construction paper, scissors, pens, pencils, erasers, and just about everything you might find in the typical kindergarten classroom. Even the lights and sound system had been outfitted to inspire creative thinking—the lights had almost a dozen settings in various colors (no disco ball, though), and the audio panel was online to play any Internet radio station through iTunes. A port on the panel also allowed anyone to plug in a flash drive or MP3 player to play their own music mixes.

"Today, we're going to work on pitching ideas," said Aaron, standing and writing the word *pitching* on one of the whiteboard surfaces. "There's a way to best pitch ideas, and how you pitch something can be just as important as the idea itself." He then wrote out a few key points on the whiteboard and explained each one.

First, he stressed the importance of knowing your audience. "Everything about your pitch," he said with emphasis, "is predicated by who you're pitching to." He went on to say that a huge portion of preparing for your pitch must include researching and understanding who will be attending—as well as those people who will perhaps review the pitch, but not attend the actual presentation.

Part of this is ascertaining who the decision-makers or opinion-leaders are. It's not always as clear as you might think. For example, an executive or manager may have an admin assistant who's highly regarded and therefore carries a lot of weight in any decision. But as the name implies, they are crucial to gaining support for your ideas because they tend to lead the pack in thinking. For a variety of reasons, they've gained the trust and respect of others when it comes to ideas, innovation, and ability to see the path before them (and the company). And it's important to understand that opinion-leaders don't necessarily hold "leader" positions within a company.

"So how do we find them and find out who they are?" Scott suddenly asked, pretty much simultaneously as he put his hand up. Scott was a definite go-getter in the company. He'd started only a year earlier as an intern out of college, but quickly earned a position as junior account exec.

"You should be telling us!" replied Aaron. Everyone laughed, knowing the impressive sales numbers Scott had already racked up. "Okay," Aaron continued, "let's say you're going after Boeing or Raytheon. Forget for the moment exactly what the sale is you're trying to make—just tell me how you'd go about scoping them out to start."

Scott hesitated for a moment, though Aaron knew he knew the answer. This was Scott's forte. And yet it was endearing that he also wasn't completely sure of his own talents. It certainly kept him from getting too cocky, as had that other intern-turned-salesman who eventually crashed and burned.

"I guess...not really knowing enough details here...I'd be looking at whatever prior sales numbers I could get for the client, or prospective client. Who bought what? Who made the final decisions? Who participated in the sales presentations? What were some of the objections? Stuff like that. Just see what worked before and how it worked."

"Exactly!" Aaron shot back. Scott couldn't restrain a smile. Aaron continued. "What worked before and how did it work and who made it work? That's the biggest part of what you ask yourself. Each of you in teams will be practicing a pitch later, which obviously won't allow you time for this reconnaissance, but you'll tell us what you would do to get this information and theoretically what the results would be."

"So, let's say I wanted a new, fancy coffee-maker for our department," said Darnella. Aaron could tell by the look in her eyes that this was something she'd been thinking about. "You know," she continued, "one of those ones with the pods. What would be best is for me, or whoever suggested the idea, to find out who all the coffee-lovers are?" Aaron started to nod when she added, "And find out who's the coffee-lover who's also the decision-maker or influencer?"

"Yep," Aaron responded.

"Like that would be hard," joked Lucas. "Mitchell spends so much time at the coffee machine he smells like Starbucks." Everyone laughed, as Mitchell was, indeed, the company's consummate coffee-drinker. "How about someone suggest Mitchell get his own coffee machine so the rest of us have a chance to get some?" Lucas earned more chuckles, as he was so good at doing.

"All right, now," Aaron interjected before it got out of hand. "Mitchell's not here to defend himself—"

"Yeah," said Meagan, "'cause he's probably at the coffee machine filling his Thermos." More laughter ensued, with a few heads shaking with thoughts of that character Mitchell. Aaron knew everyone liked the guy, so he wasn't worried that things were getting ugly. Mitchell, a middle-level manager in logistics, was impossible not to like. Though he was still in his 40s, he had a way about him that made him much older—probably because he brought a brown-bag lunch in his briefcase every day and always wore a tie even though he never left the office. He was a master at self-deprecating humor and gave himself plenty of material, apparently not having bought any new clothes since 1987. And although he wasn't the deepest thinker (based on a typical conversation, he clearly watched dozens of TV shows on a regular basis), he never maintained anything less than an infectiously positive attitude.

"Ahem," said Aaron in a mock clearing of his throat. "Where were we? Ah yes, Darnella's coffee-pod-maker pitch. Yes, Darnella, you're exactly right. Who loves coffee and has the influence to do something about it? That's a big thing you would need to find out. But the 'who' is only part of the equation. Let's move on to the next key thing to remember."

With that, Aaron wrote on the board:

It's not about you or your idea—it's about your audience.

The most successful pitches, he elaborated, are those done with the audience in mind. This is why it's so critical to carefully and clearly identify these people first. If you don't know who they are, how can you know what will benefit, interest, or excite them? Though it would've been easy, Aaron avoided using Mitchell again as an example. Instead he asked about another manager, Barbara, who works in marketing: "Those of you who know her, what do you think would be a benefit to keep in mind if you were pitching her? Don't worry about what the pitch is, just what makes her tick."

There were four people in the meeting who knew Barbara well enough to answer. They were thinking about it for a few moments before Chad chimed in.

"She's a perfectionist. She likes to make sure all the i's are dotted and the t's are crossed."

"Good," Aaron said. "And what does this tell you about pitching something to her? Kimberly?" Kimberly had her hand raised; she'd worked in marketing under Barbara for almost two years before transferring to sales.

"She's afraid of mistakes. I don't mean to say something mean, but she more than anything wants to make sure something is right. She would triple-check files before they went to the printer. I'm not saying it's a bad thing. It's not. So, if you were to pitch something to her, you better make sure it's well done and there are no typos or anything like that."

"But dig deeper," Aaron said. "What would you have to convey in your pitch to bring her aboard?"

"Um..." Kimberly thought about it. "I guess, security?"

"Exactly," responded Aaron. He knew Barbara enough to know this was her key motivator. Of course, everyone likes and needs security, but we all do to different extents. Barbara's desire for security was definitely at the high end of the spectrum. "And it's not just job security," he continued. "She wants to make sure things go smoothly, that there's no chaos. And I'm not saying anything she doesn't already know or I wouldn't say if she were here in the room. We could all guess psychologically why this is, but the bottom line is, it just is. So, any pitch to her would have to include—an absolute must—everything necessary to show that it's a safe idea that's been thought through with every possible contingency planned for."

Quite a few people at the table were taking notes. Many of the others nodded in interest. Even those who didn't know Barbara got the concept. What is the key thing that drives the decision-maker? Who in the company, besides that person, would know this? Is there a way to figure it out from the person's actions and behavior? Once again, it comes back to knowing the person as much as possible before making any pitch.

"And this brings us to the next point," Aaron said, moving back to the whiteboard wall. "Anticipate and be prepared for objections or challenges." He paused while everyone wrote it down. "Even when you're not dealing with someone like Barbara, everyone in a position of decision-making is going to be concerned about what might go wrong. They have to be. It's their butts on the line when something does go wrong."

Aaron went on to explain that it's important to have a least one "negative monkey" in your Wild Idea Club. The negative monkey has the task of finding flaws in any pitch, idea, or plan. These people are usually those who lean toward being negative, doubtful, or suspicious by nature. Rather than trying to force everyone into a positive mode (which can often be resisted by negative monkeys who see wild-eyed optimism as a nice but unrealistic ideal), take advantage of those who see the glass as half empty. (Probably best, however, to avoid those who think the glass has been poisoned.)

Aaron had started using the phrase "negative monkeys" after learning about an interesting study on a TV nature show. Scientists were researching a colony of monkeys in the wild, and through careful observation had noted that approximately 10 percent of them were negative. They exhibited negative behavior and were very much like their "glass is half empty" human counterparts. The scientists then wondered how the colony would change if the negative monkeys were removed. How were these monkeys keeping the others down? How were they "poisonous" to the mental health and enjoyment of the colony? So, the researchers removed the negative monkeys from the colony for a few months and then came back to see the results. To their astonishment, and sadly, the rest of the colony was dead. They'd apparently been murdered by a rival colony. The researchers quickly realized the negative monkeys served a vital purpose—as an early-warning signal. Because they perceived things suspiciously, cautiously, and sensed danger when the "positive monkeys" did not, they were necessary to the survival of the colony.

Aaron paused for a moment as the club soaked in the lesson. He knew from telling this story a number of times before that it was fascinating to people and they often needed time to process it—especially because it goes counter to the popular positive-thinking mantra usually taught in corporate training.

"So again," he continued, "harness the perception of the negative monkeys. Let them show the group the flaws and holes in your pitch. It's a vital function. But in addition to them, make sure you also have troubleshooters to fix the flaws. These are people who are natural improvers. They thrive on challenges and can usually find solutions when others are stuck. When you hear someone who often says, 'Here's how we can do that better,' that's usually a troubleshooter type. Ideally, every Wild Idea Club should have at least one negative monkey and troubleshooter. For the purposes of our practice pitches today, however, because there are only three people in each team, you might not have a negative monkey and troubleshooter. So, just do your best to function in those roles in your teams."

"Is that monkey story really true?" asked Kimberly. Ironically, as soon as she asked this, Aaron knew she was a negative monkey. They rarely believe anything they hear unless it's been verified, and he suspected she'd go back to her desk later and Google the story.

"Yes, it is, believe it or not," answered Aaron. "Now, I might be wrong about them being monkeys. I saw this a few years ago, and maybe they were chimps. But the concept still holds true."

Aaron stepped over to the nearby soda fountain before he continued. Although it did have your standard variety of soda choices, this machine was unique to this conference room because it also had a couple choices of energy drinks—useful for long idea sessions. Aaron opted, however, for the healthier green tea.

"Okay, there are a few more key things to know before we take a break." He then wrote two words on the board: *senses* and *short*.

Repeatedly tapping the board where he wrote *senses*, he explained how our brains process information through all of our senses, not just listening and watching. But he also explained how we can heighten the use of the auditory and visual senses—because we use them so much, they can often be dulled. In fact, his tapping on the board was one technique to sharpen the auditory sense. By tapping on the word as people read it, he added a "marker" in their minds to help store the information.

"Darnella, let's go back to your coffee-machine pitch," he said. "This would be a clear example of a situation in which you could engage all the senses. If it were me, I'd make sure the coffee machine you're pitching was in the room. Have it brewing for the smell. Pass around the pods for everyone to touch and smell. And then, of course, pass out samples of the coffee once it's ready."

"But how would I get the machine?" she asked, clearly working this plan in her mind.

"That's what the Wild Idea Club is for," Aaron responded. "If you were serious about pursuing this, you could form a Wild Idea Club just for this purpose. Remember, these clubs don't have to be ongoing; they can be started for one particular reason. But you'll often find they keep on going, because there are always other ideas that come up."

Lucas couldn't resist a wisecrack: "Hey, Darnella, just go to Target and buy it for the pitch. Then, if your idea isn't approved, you have 90 days to return it." A couple of people in the room shot him a disapproving look. "What?" he mock protested. "Is that against the law?"

"Okay," Aaron stepped in. "So, you get the gist of it. Engage the senses. Let your Wild Idea Club come up with ways to make this happen, especially when it's not as easy as a coffee idea."

The last point before the break was the importance of keeping pitches as short as possible. Aaron acknowledged the fine line it is: You want to engage everyone sufficiently, but you also don't want to take up their time and remind them they could be doing other things. And this is especially true as you go up the decision-maker ladder, where typically people get busier and busier and their time is even shorter.

One way to establish a good length for your pitch is to let the key decision-maker who'll be attending the presentation decide in advance. Then, design your pitch to not just fit within the time frame, but be much shorter. This is a clever technique because it allows for a number of benefits. One, if things go off track, you'll have spare time. Two, if the attendees (especially the key decision-maker) are very engaged, you'll have extra time to hash out their interests or concerns. And three, if your pitch ends and the additional minutes aren't needed, everyone is appreciative of the extra time.

The group quickly jotted down their notes, some no doubt pressured by their bladders. Aaron watched over everyone to make sure each person got their notes down. A lot of facilitators at that point would've asked if there were any questions. But Aaron knew it was smarter to let them take their break; otherwise, the people who are fidgety will either tune out or tend to resent the questions. Plus, the time during the break often generates questions that can be answered afterward.

"Okay, let's break for 10 minutes. When we come back, you'll all split into your teams and develop a pitch based on what we just learned. And then we'll end the meeting with the pitches and critiques. Sound good?" Everyone nodded and smiled with genuine enthusiasm, and Aaron couldn't have been happier.

"And by the way, you're welcome to leave your hats here if you don't want to walk around the office as a Doofus or Boner." After a few chuckles, not surprisingly, everyone put their hats on the table—everyone except, of course, Lucas.

Chapter Six
The Start of Something Big

If I have seen further, it is by standing on the shoulders of giants. —Sir Isaac Newton

Danielle "Danny" Fox opened the door to her hotel room with a hint of hesitancy. But it wasn't out of worry; it was curiosity. She'd been coming to this hotel for years on her travels as an author and professional speaker, and it was with great anticipation that she had awaited the renovation.

And this wasn't just any renovation—the kind that usually means new carpeting, replacing clunky TVs with flat-screens, or offering a menu of shampoos. Icarus Hotels, a growing regional chain that caters to business travelers, was rolling out a "boutique floor." This floor, dedicated to solo business travelers, featured many innovations, the most talked-about being the rooms themselves.

Danny wheeled her carry-on bag behind her as she slowly stepped into the room, a look of astonishment on her face. The mid-afternoon sunlight streamed in through the sheer curtains, behind which she could see the geometric shapes of the buildings immediately to the west. The traffic some 20 stories below on West 56th Street was only a memory now as the impressively soundproofed room contained nothing more than the quiet, welcoming sounds of a satellite-radio jazz station playing through unseen speakers. A few months earlier, Danny had wondered why the hotel asked on a questionnaire what music she likes.

The aspect of this new boutique floor generating the most publicity was the size of the rooms. Roughly half the size of a typical hotel room, they were marvels of efficiency. As the hotel studied the needs of its target guests for such a renovation, they found they typically stayed only one or two nights, spent little time in the room except to sleep, carried very little in the way of clothes or accessories, and spent most of their in-room time either on the Internet or watching TV. As such, gone were the excessively large wardrobe closets and three-drawer dressers; in their place a small closet featuring one drawer and a pull-out trouser-press. The coffee-service area and mini-bar were cleverly replaced with a smaller version built into the wall beneath the mounted flat-screen TV. On the adjacent wall, a simple desktop hung from hinges—as you lifted it away from the wall, two thin legs folded down to the floor. Pull up the nearby rolling chair and, *voilà*, you have your desk area to work.

It was probably a full minute before Danny noticed there was no bed. Well, more accurately, it was there but she just didn't realize it—in the form of a Murphy bed that could be pulled down from the wall. With this discovery, she nodded with a slight smile, revealing her awe and approval. Best of all, these "micro rooms" allowed her to stay in Manhattan at half the price of what she was typically spending to visit. "Why pay for space you don't need?" was the headline in an e-mail newsletter she had received from Icarus Hotels a couple of months prior.

Downstairs in the office, Alexis Eckers broke into a smile of her own, perhaps telepathically picking up on the satisfaction of one of her best guests upstairs. Since the rollout of the boutique floor, things had been going very well. Not a week went by in which she wasn't being interviewed by an in-flight magazine, one of the industry publications, or a paper or magazine in the city. Though she was the general manager at the Midtown property, she made sure to never take all the credit in any interview—in fact, it was with great pride that she'd reveal the source of the boutique-floor idea: one of their housekeepers.

It was nearly two years earlier that Alexis was interviewing Maria Lopez, a 37-year-old mother of four who had emigrated from El Salvador and settled in New York City with her extended family. The interview was not for a job, but rather a regular interview that Alexis did to keep a pulse on every aspect of the hotel. And it was during that interview that Maria was asked what she thought would make the hotel better and the guests happier.

"You know, Ms. Eckers, my English is no so good for the speaking," Maria had said. "But I do listen and hear what the guests are saying." She went on to explain how many of them were lamenting the cost of hotel stays, especially in Manhattan. In some cases, their businesses were looking to cut costs (which possibly meant these guests would be staying in New Jersey). In other cases, the travelers were self-employed (as is Danny) and looking to keep more money in their pockets or extend their stays. And in nearly every case, it was obvious to Maria that they neither used nor needed a 350-square-foot hotel room.

Alexis had been stunned at the serendipity of this conversation. The hotel was planning an overhaul of a few of the upper floors the following year, and this could be an opportunity for the taking. *What if we could put double the rooms on those floors*, she had thought in that moment, *and charge 60 percent of the rates for the current rooms?* That would be a win–win. Although there was a lot to consider and research, something about the concept felt good in her gut.

"Have you heard of our Wild Idea Club?" had been her next question to Maria.

♀ ♀ ♀

Back in the present, Alexis was interrupted by her phone. It was Darryl Hodge, a former kitchen worker in the hotel restaurant who had been promoted to oversee the catering services on the boutique floor. Before Alexis recruited Maria for the hotel's Wild Idea Club, there had been only four people involved, mostly coming up with smaller ideas, but once Alexis brought the boutique-floor idea into the club, she added numerous other employees into the group in addition to Maria. The idea was big enough that it would need far more than four club members. There were details upon details that needed to not just be sorted out and implemented, but also thought about from fresh, creative angles. This was where Darryl came in.

Having been in the kitchen for nearly a year, he was always coming up with ideas anyhow, primarily increasing efficiency during the meals. But some were also cost-cutters. For example, he'd noticed that most people were cutting their carbs and only eating one of the two breadsticks served with salads. He suggested only serving the one. Besides avoiding this waste, he suspected this could save the kitchen a decent amount of money in a year, and he was right. Alexis knew his innovative mind would match well with the new floor concept, and she wasn't let down. It was in their Wild Idea Club's third meeting that Darryl had suggested essentially bringing a bistro to the boutique floor—primarily catering to the floor's guests with a limited menu of items, a breakfast-on-the-go package, a bag lunch, and evening munchies and drinks. The bistro ultimately was built in what had been a corner guest room next to the elevators. A European facade now wrapped around that corner, with old-world windows and warm interior lighting inviting guests into the café.

Now, nearly any day of the week, Darryl could be found in his creation, tending to various aspects of it with the pride of ownership. This was one of the keys to successfully executing ideas for Alexis and her Wild Idea Club. When someone was given not only credit for an idea, but also ownership of it, the person's involvement and level of job satisfaction increased immensely. Alexis was acutely aware of how many other hotels had employees who clocked in and out every day, simply doing their jobs during the hours in between. This was not to say every Icarus employee was whistling while they work like something out of a 1940s musical, but survey after survey found them to be far more content there than they had been at other hotels. And the turnover rate was significantly less than the industry standard. By assigning each employee ownership for his or her idea, whether small or big, Alexis built a culture of pride and commitment. It was with this mindset that Darryl had called Alexis.

"We're not going to be able to carry the blueberry muffins anymore," he told her with a tone of apology and regret.

"Why not?"

"I just got off the phone with the supplier in Queens, and they told me the bakery is closing."

"That's awful," responded Alexis. These were no ordinary blueberry muffins. They were organically made, with blueberries grown at a farm in Connecticut. Their freshness was incomparable, and guests frequently bought extra muffins to ship home. "Why is the bakery closing?"

"They told me the owner died and his son doesn't want to run the business," Darryl said. "It's possible they'll find a buyer, but for the time being, they're taking a break while the family mourns."

"Let's send them a card," said Alexis. "And I guess you'll have to start shopping around for a replacement."

"That's exactly why I'm calling. We'll most likely not have enough for tomorrow morning, so I was thinking I could check out some places this afternoon before they close. There's a good place in SoHo and another in the West Village; I could stop there before I catch the train home."

"Of course, Darryl. Is Vida there for the evening?"

"Yes, she got here at 3:30. So, we're covered."

"Okay. As soon as you're ready, you can take off. Stop by on your way out and I'll give you the Visa card to make a purchase for at least tomorrow. And then we'll go from there."

💡 💡 💡

Later that evening, Danny was perusing the DVDs in the hotel library. She'd just finished dinner and wanted to chill out for the evening, and a movie was exactly what she wanted. She couldn't believe the hotel now had a library when she'd read about it in the in-room guide. It was long ago that she'd quit ordering pay-per-view movies through the hotel room TV—specifically when they hit $9.95 a pop. And some hotels were charging $12.95. To her, that was just robbery, and more often than not, she regretted the money spent because the movie wasn't as good as she'd hoped.

"Oh my God," she said out loud. "I can't believe this is here." She was holding a copy of *Over the Edge*, a movie she hadn't seen since junior high school many years ago.

"Whatcha find?" said the clerk, curiously peering over from the counter.

"*Over the Edge!*" Danny answered, holding up the DVD case incredulously. "Do you know this movie?"

"Yeah, I picked it. Awesome flick."

"Really? You know this movie?" Danny said as the clerk came over. "Wow. Most people have never heard of it."

"That's partly why I did. I want this place to be a mix of what people are looking for—you know, like *Ocean's Eleven* or a Will Smith movie—and some surprises, like what you've got."

"So, you're the manager here?" Danny asked.

"Yeah, I guess you can call me that. I came up with the idea to have a place here in the hotel where people could pick up a cool movie or book or even a CD and take it back to their room."

Danny looked around, suddenly noticing the bookshelves and CD racks. *How cool!* she thought. "And so they let you run the place? That's great."

"Yeah," the clerk responded with a smile and a slight lift in her stance. "The hotel is excellent. A lot of us have had ideas, and then, if it's possible to work out, they let us run them. It's awesome."

Danny was fascinated by what she was hearing. She had traveled all 50 states and a dozen other countries in the past several years. She was a true road warrior. And she knew from staying in countless hotels how few were on to something similar to what she was discovering here. The Midtown Manhattan Icarus was excellent when she'd last been there a few months before, but now it was in a league of its own.

For the next 10 minutes or so, Danny and the clerk had the library to themselves, and Danny grilled her on how this all came to be. The clerk, who finally introduced herself as Anna, gave Danny a quick tutorial on the Wild Idea Club concept—she had clearly been indoctrinated well. She said it's all about follow-through and accountability. The hotel had heard a number of great ideas from its employees (and guests) throughout the years, but more often than not, they never came to fruition. Usually, they would slowly die, like a plant without water, until they were forgotten. Once Alexis had become general manager and started the Wild Idea Club, she stressed the importance of following through on all ideas that were agreed to be feasible. Yes, Anna said, sometimes ideas eventually proved to be impractical, but even those ideas were put into a special book in Alexis's office, in case they were resurrected in the future.

"How do you all keep the follow-through going?" Danny asked. She knew that in any organization, any structure of human resources, this was usually the most challenging thing.

"It's like the government—there are checks and balances." Danny couldn't believe she was hearing this. Far too many of the hotel employees she'd encountered were dead-eyed workers who, even when they had a smile on their faces, obviously didn't want to be there. This Anna was positively alive in her work. "So, for example, whatever idea we come up with, if it's implemented, we have a team of people on it, even if it's just two or three of us. And get this: the person who came up with the idea gets to pick the team. But they have to justify why they've picked their teammates. It can't be just for personal reasons."

"So what about your library here?" Danny asked. "What team do you have?"

"Well, there are just four of us. I picked a guy named Carsten because he used to work in a real library when he was in college and liked it. Then, I picked a woman named Delphia, because she's great with people, and another guy, Allen, who just wanted to be part of it 'cause he thinks it's cool."

"So they all work in here too?"

"We all rotate with our other jobs here. I mostly work front desk, Allen is a valet and bellhop the rest of the time, Carsten is a concierge, and Delphia is in the restaurant."

"Well, that's not bad," Danny said. "I guess it helps you keep from getting bored."

"Totally. I mean, the front desk is not bad, but this breaks up the day when I'm in here. Plus, it's like my own thing." Anna was nodding in affirmation of her own statement when she suddenly added, "Oh, and guess what! We get to have weekly meetings, just me and my team!"

At first, Danny was a little puzzled by the comment. After all, most people view work meetings as an unnecessary distraction and waste of time. To hear Anna, all of probably 25 years old, expressing genuine enthusiasm about meetings was, well, weird. Danny asked her why she liked the meetings so much.

"Well, think about it. People are social creatures, right? But what do most work places try to do? Cut out socializing. But here, we're actually encouraged to have weekly meetings on our teams, even if it's just two people. I'm not saying we goof off or anything, but it's just good to get to talk some, away from your actual work. But the truth is, we get a lot done and we feel like we're working on something important."

If Danny wasn't impressed before, she certainly was now. This was an amazing story. Anna went on to tell her about Lupe, a Guatemalan immigrant who works in the hotel with her sister, Marcella. After going to an outdoor market in Chelsea where she saw a vendor selling specialty handmade soaps, Lupe suggested the hotel sell them. And similar to the blueberry muffins in Darryl's bistro, these were no ordinary soaps—the person who created them was a true artisan from Old Europe. So Lupe was authorized to set up a kiosk in the lobby as a test to see how they would sell, and she had her sister join her in the in-house venture. "She rocked!" Anna said. The soaps were a huge hit, and as a result, Lupe and Marcella now go to the outdoor market every Thursday—on the clock—and shop for more soaps. "So, do you think they're going to be quitting the hotel anytime soon?" Anna asked, almost rhetorically.

"No," Danny responded quietly, stunned at a story that was as equally interesting as Anna's library. Little did she know the whole boutique floor had come from the mind of one of the housekeepers as well.

Just then, Anna noticed another guest waiting at the counter to check out a couple of CDs. She excused herself as Danny contemplated what she'd just heard. It was genius—a phenomenal example of bringing out the best in people. And no doubt it was a gold mine of publicity. The last few times she'd stayed there, little did she know what was cooking behind the scenes. Suddenly, she remembered the DVD in her hand and went to the counter. Anna had just finished with the other guest.

"Anna, it was nice to meet you," Danny said. "And gosh...what can I say? This is a great thing you have here. Congratulations. Thank you for thinking of it and making it happen."

"You're welcome, Danny. Great to meet you as well." She scanned the DVD, and then asked Danny for her key card to put the rental on her room account. As long as she returned it the next day, there would be no charge. Or, Anna explained, she could choose to keep it and the $20 fee would be added to her bill at checkout.

"Really?" Danny was thinking seriously about that, since she'd been wanting to add *Over the Edge* to her collection.

"Yep. In fact, we do a fair amount of business selling the DVDs, books, and CDs. People often want them for the plane ride home, or sometimes they just like them that much."

Danny nodded and said, "See you soon" as she headed back to her room. But first, she thought it might be a good idea to stop at Lupe's soap kiosk.

Chapter Seven
Honk if You're an Innovative Thinker

Every person who ends up buying into your idea does so by changing it into his idea—even if it looks a lot like your idea.
—Tom Peters

Every CEO will tell you it is through innovation that their company survives and thrives. This could be in the form of new products and services or cost-cutting and efficiency. But how many companies *truly* dedicate themselves to innovation? For many, what's lacking is a systematic way to seed, cultivate, and harvest the crop of ideas that continually grow. First, you need a forum for idea generation and development, a system to capture ideas, and a process to test and possibly turn them into reality quickly and efficiently. (This is where the Wild Idea Club comes in.) Second, you need to use technology to get ideas from your people and allow more employees to share and build on their ideas with each other. (This is where the Internet, communication gadgets, and social networking come in.)

The concept that ideas are everywhere has never been truer. Today, largely due to the Internet and information boom, the next big idea (and many good small ones) can come from customers, suppliers, or literally anyone in your company. This is especially true of today's younger workers. Their generation has grown up with a strong sense of self, identity, and expression. They've lived most of their memorable lives in a society that caters to the individual—whether it's Burger King's "Have it your way," the ability to create your own channel on YouTube, or being able to have a blog that can get noticed by the mainstream media. This strong sense of self and expression can be harnessed for greater good by getting them involved and soliciting their ideas.

But people of all ages and backgrounds respond to expression and involvement. This is why it's so important to create a culture in which wild ideas are not just heard but implemented when warranted. And everything can be improved when you give credit where credit is due—believing in the collective creativity and resourcefulness of your people.

Many employees care about the company they work for (or what it provides) and want to give it their all, but feel as though they are working with one hand tied behind their backs because there are so many barriers to being able to do their jobs. If you give these people on the front lines a chance to improve the product or their own productivity, they will reward you handsomely for your trust in them. Let them collaborate, contribute, and come up with solutions, and you will see a big boost in their morale and the bottom line. Create a climate of creativity and encourage everyone to share their ideas.

As it turns out, in our examination of the most innovative companies, we have found that many of the best (and most profitable) ideas have come from the people who are knee deep in the work and close to the customer. They have hundreds of ideas and just need someone to listen to them, a system to submit them, and a way to get them implemented.

Collaboration and Wild Idea Clubs increase the awareness of what everyone does (and appreciation as well). If everyone is involved and represented, from the customers to the cooks, you get a true sense of what's going on, and what the needs are across the board.

The goal is that great ideas not get left behind. To reach that goal, remember, the more ideas the better, and ideas can come from anywhere in the organization. The key is to have everyone's ideas heard. It doesn't matter where an idea comes from; if it's good, it's good, whether the person who submitted it has an MBA or not. Every idea could be a plus for your organization, and you encourage them by soliciting everyone and giving their ideas due consideration.

But coming up with ideas is only half the battle. It takes a leader's willingness to implement them. If not, these ideas are wasted and your people will stop trying. It's not easy to be the kind of manager or owner who culls ideas from your employees and then turns the best of them into reality. There is a chance everyone involved can look silly, or worse, lose money. Trying out new ideas is like riding a motorcycle: There are those who have crashed, and those who will. But on the flip side, if you don't embrace your employees' ideas, they might just take those ideas elsewhere—like to your competitors.

The bigger the company, historically the harder it is for it to embrace the concept of collaboration; as the saying goes, the bigger you are, the harder you fall. Smaller companies foster collaboration out of necessity, and big organizations need to get with the program as well. If they don't use a collaborative approach to solving simple problems, they will suffer in most every area: innovation, service, product and development, employee morale, and communication. And as business cycles get faster and faster, having a streamlined innovation process becomes all the more imperative.

The positive effect of Wild Idea Clubs goes both ways— from the bottom up and the top down. Everyone benefits as the results boost productivity and profits. Employees become problem-solvers in their workplace and benefit directly from an improved work environment and higher morale. Conversely, managers love to have people come to them with ideas rather than complaints, and can be rewarded for better oversight of their departments.

No matter what your company's size or industry is, seriously consider whether your methods of innovation are as good as they can be,. In today's business world, where ideas can fly at the speed of an e-mail or text message and employees function in a state of free agency, companies that don't embrace employee innovation are in serious danger of extinction. What follows is an inspirational look at how many successful companies, from small to huge, have rediscovered the power of their people.

3M

You may not know that the ubiquitous Post-It note was invented by someone named Art Fry while he was employed by 3M. Fry was at church and looking for a safe way to mark his book of hyms without damaging the pages, and *voila*, the Post-It Note was created. The interesting thing was, many at 3M didn't get it at first and rejected his new idea. So Fry made sure everyone saw the Post-It Note's potential by having them used on inter-office memos—and the rest is history.

Since 1902 (when William L. McKnight took over) the corporation has encouraged creative thinking and looked for employees with an entrepreneurial spirit. Through the decades, the company has embraced teamwork and collaboration when it comes to developing new ideas. 3M prides itself on innovative teams and fostering a safe environment where individuals with wild ideas are welcomed and where creative genius is rewarded.

AMAZON.COM

Many times companies that embrace creative collaboration and wild ideas do so because those in charge are big believers themselves. Amazon.com's Jeff Bezos is certainly someone who believes in innovation, and the company has benefited from many of their own breakthroughs, such as one-click shopping (faster checkout), their associates program (revenue sharing), and of course, Kindle (a portable reader for electronic books). One of the ways Bezos and his brain trust innovate is by focusing on the needs of their customers. He has also taken a lot of heat from Wall Street for putting his pioneering ahead of quarterly profits.

AMERICAN AIRLINES

American Airlines is a big believer in encouraging employee ideas—especially because their "IdeAAs in Flight" idea-management program has saved the carrier nearly $600 million dollars since 1987 and generates nearly 20,000 ideas each year. Perhaps most famous is the story of eliminating olives from salads (because 72 percent of the passengers weren't eating them) and saving half a million dollars the first year from that one move alone. In another instance, a warehouse in St. Thomas, Virgin Islands, that served as overnight storage for shipped valuables was constantly being burglarized. American cut its expensive security contract there, replacing it with a tape recording of a dog randomly barking. It worked.

Perhaps most impressive is the program's employee rewards for cost-saving ideas. In one instance, a flight attendant's suggestion reduced the annual cost of caviar served in first class by $567,000; she was awarded $50,000. When a mechanic noticed the company was being charged two different prices for an identical part (because they were being used on two different kinds of planes), the resulting savings were estimated at $300,000, and he was awarded $37,500 for his observation. And yet another mechanic received $50,000 for successfully identifying and demonstrating a costly maintenance step that was being done far more often than needed.

APPLE

Apple is clearly one of the most innovative companies around today. Not only has Apple (and founder Steve Jobs) changed the way we use our computers, but the company has also been instrumental in revolutionizing the way we browse, buy, and listen to music (iTunes and the iPod), as well as how we view the phone (iPhone).

We can surmise that Jobs is the mastermind behind many of these incredible ideas. And we can assume that he is surrounded by other big thinkers at Apple who also want to change the world (for the better) one innovation at a time. It's refreshing to see products with good design, easy-to-use interfaces, and outstanding performance that dominate their niche. Add to that a retail experience like no other at Apple's stores, and you get one of the world's most innovative and successful companies.

Because Apple is so secretive about its creative processes, we can only look at the output and wonder how they keep coming up with such great stuff. But we can get a glimpse from an interview with Steve Jobs (*BusinessWeek*, October 12, 2004), in which he says, "It's ad hoc meetings of six people called by someone who thinks he has figured out the coolest new thing ever and who wants to know what other people think of his idea."

BEST BUY

Best Buy implemented a new Results-Only Work Environment program (ROWE) to create an atmosphere where productivity is more important than the hours worked. The idea to allow Best Buy employees to work when and where they want (as long as they get their work done) came from a group of employees who believed (rightly) that this would increase productivity and morale and reduce stress and turnover—and it's worked. ROWE grew from the bottom up at Best Buy because the people who proposed it were passionate and got others on board by brainstorming with key coworkers virally.

BMW

When BMW launched its Virtual Innovation Agency (VIA) to canvass suggestions from people all round the world it received 4,000 ideas in the first week. And they continue to roll in.

BOEING

Many employers forbid their employees from blogging (Virgin Airlines is one example), but Boeing is using the format as a way to gain valuable feedback from their customers, the public, and—surprise—their employees. The aerospace giant has found that having a dialogue with those outside the company is an excellent way to generate ideas. They also use blogs internally to give employees a forum to (anonymously) raise concerns and offer solutions and suggestions.

COUNCIL OF HOTEL AND RESTAURANT TRAINERS

Nonprofit CHART is one of the oldest groups dedicated to the trade. But the group's 600-plus members have a new trick up their sleeve: They're using state-of-the-art technology to share the latest training practices, innovations, solutions to problems—just about anything. "Ask My Peers" is an online listserv that connects the CHART community to hundreds of members with years of expertise. Those who join can e-mail top-of-mind training and human resource challenges to the community and quickly receive feedback from entrepreneurs to multi-unit operators. Recent queries focused on new hire retention, manager training, and computer-based education. Discussions are archived on the Website, *www.chart.org*, and are searchable by topic. The service has grown so popular that CHART is introducing "Ask My Peers: LIVE" at its semi-annual hospitality training conferences this year.

CRAIGSLIST

If you aren't familiar with Craigslist, chances are you haven't sold anything online in the past few years—it is the number-one classified service in any medium, with millions of people posting free ads for just about anything and everything (within reason) every month. What's amazing about the success of the company, founded by Craig Newmark in 1995, is how it has grown with ideas and insights coming from those using the service.

What was initially started as a hobby by Newmark (in e-mail format), featuring San Francisco event listings, soon became so popular that it quickly grew to include a Web interface within a year.

First, Newmark decided how it could best be used. Then, people trying to fill technical positions found that the list was a good way to reach people with the skills they were looking for. This led to the addition of a category for jobs. User demand caused the list of categories to grow. And it was about this time that community members started asking for a Web interface. Newmark enlisted the help of volunteers and contractors to create a Website user interface for the different mailing list categories.

The workplace Newmark created was intentionally non-corporate, with no cubicles or dress codes. He had spent many years working in places that were highly structured, and, as a result, took to a more anti-authoritarian style. By eliminating nearly all of the standard corporate constraints (deadlines, time cards, micro-management, and so on) that inhibit creativity, the result is an environment where people actually feel good about coming to work. But more than anything, Newmark attributes the success to hiring the right people in the first place. "Once we have people who fit that description," he said, "I've always found that it is just a matter of letting them do their work."

DAPHNE'S GREEK CAFE

Daphne's Greek Cafe was founded in 1991 by George Katakalidis in San Diego. He now has restaurants throughout California, Arizona, Oregon, and Colorado. Part of the reason for the rapid rise to success—Daphne's is the largest fast-casual Greek restaurant chain in the United States—is management's openness to new ideas generated by employees on the front lines.

Katakalidis says, "I truly believe every employee has a wild idea or two from time to time, and entrepreneurs probably every minute. I like to ideate by group and get as much feedback as possible so I can validate the thought process."

He also prefers his people get their ideas to him any way they can, and admits many times he hears about them in casual conversation. He then asks the employee to follow up by putting the idea in writing and sending it to him.

"Once perused," Katakalidis continues, "if it warrants more detail I ask for a detailed presentation to the group, in a management meeting. Most of the ideas that have helped us grow are proposed as a trial balloon in our central management meetings, and then tested to see if they will work. If they do, we start rolling it out."

Katakalidis likes his people to show initiative and solve problems with creative thinking—and gives them some latitude and leeway to do so. "One instance where an employee used resourcefulness and good judgment involved a makeshift curbside delivery. One of our locations in Los Angeles has poor parking. A customer called and said he couldn't park, but had a hankering for one of our signature dishes. So the GM came out, delivered the food, and handled the transaction right on the street."

DEL TACO

The 500-restaurant chain founded in 1961 holds an annual employee recipe contest. Employees are invited to enter dishes produced with ingredients found in the company's kitchens (plus one additional ingredient). Winners receive cash prices, and their entries are considered as possible new menu items.

DIGITAL RIVER

This e-commerce leader has a CEO, Joel Ronning, who seriously believes in the power of employee ideas. The company holds weekly "entrepreneur councils" with employees to search for new and improved ways to increase sales and reduce costs. These meetings have proven to be very productive and have helped the company generate ideas worth hundreds of thousands of dollars—with cash prizes awarded to employees for the best ideas. The company tries to create a corporate culture of creativity (and fun) by allowing dogs at work once a month and hosts quarterly lunches where employees can exchange ideas with Ronning.

DISNEY

In 1952, Imagineering (imagination and engineering) was a company formed by Walt Disney and made up of a diverse group of people chartered with designing and building the company's signature theme park. Throughout the years, Imagineers have been instrumental in developing many of the ideas used at Disney's parks. The Wild Idea Club relevance is the wide range of Imagineers working together—engineers, artists, architects, writers, set designers, construction managers, and computer programmers. The results have been some of the most beloved attractions in the parks (It's A Small World and

Pirates of the Caribbean are two examples). The diverse group has the creative brainpower to conjure up wild ideas and the technical expertise to see them to completion. Imagineers were insulated from the "real world" and worked in their own way and at their own pace. Eventually, Disney decided they wanted more creative output for less money and set up a more developed system for ideation (and completion), but also allowed the Imagineers to come up with anything that would help grow the company.

eBAY

A few dozen eBay employees decided one day over pizza to form a green team to find creative ways to lessen their impact on the environment. The results are more people involved (more than 1,000 members at 10 locations) and fewer people using Styrofoam, paper plates, and plastic utensils (and other improvements as well). The green teams work independently and brainstorm ideas for new ways to become more environmentally aware. (It should be noted that Yahoo! also has a green team, which brought about several significant changes, including setting all of its copy machines to print on both sides of the paper, thus cutting paper consumption at the Internet giant in half.)

FOX'S PIZZA DEN

Prices at the gas pump in 2008 really walloped the delivery guys. That's why Pittsburgh-based Fox's Pizza Den instituted a couple of strategies to help its drivers, and itself. With "pick-up only" discount specials, customers who come in their own car on Mondays and Tuesdays get a large one-topping pie for $6.99—a savings over the $10.80 regular price. Despite the deep discount, the program works out pretty well, says Jim Fox, Jr., VP of the 250-unit chain. "Our check on those nights isn't $6.99," he says. "People are coming in and picking other things—salads, hoagies, an extra pie. Our average ticket on those otherwise normally slow days is still well over $15."

When pump prices skyrocketed that summer, Fox's instituted a $1 delivery charge. "Customers didn't blink an eye," he notes. "Fuel's crazy, everybody's eating it." The dollar goes right to the drivers.

GEORGIA-PACIFIC

Idea-management software is one way to tap into the creativity of employees and generate ideas for new products and services (as well as a way to cut costs). Georgia-Pacific has saved millions of dollars and developed products and processes using powerful computer-brainstorming tools to connect people (and pull ideas) from all areas of the company. With more than 50,000 employees (many of whom have worked there for more than two decades), there are a lot of ideas floating around. By using a form of virtual brainstorming, the company now has a way to capture and develop them.

According to an article in *InformationWeek* (March 23, 2005), Georgia-Pacific was able to cut $1.2 million a year from production costs just on paper towels the company manufactures. The idea came from a mill worker who suggested a less-expensive process for making the cardboard tubes inside paper towel rolls, during an idea-generation event (using Idea Central software) for 16,000 paper-towel-product employees. Employees who participate are rewarded points for every idea they submit, and these points can then be redeemed for prizes.

GOOGLE

It shouldn't come as a surprise that software giant Google embraces wild ideas, considering that their unconventional Mountain View, California, campus features almost everything an employee could ask for—and then some. They can have their car washed and oil changed, drop off the kids at daycare, take their dog for a walk, have a gourmet lunch, play a game of beach volleyball, attend a yoga class, and catch a few winks in a nap pod—all without leaving work. The ideas for many of these on-site perks came from the employees themselves.

In addition to a convenient and healthy workplace, many employees are interested in being environmentally responsible too, and Google listened. The company makes bicycles available to employees for getting from building to building, and draws a good percentage of its power from solar panels. No wonder they were ranked first in *Fortune* magazine's 2008 list of the best U.S. companies to work for.

Yes, many of us would love to work for a company with half of Google's perks (and the pay is good too), but what makes this such a special place is a corporate culture where new ideas are appreciated, rewarded, and enacted. In many ways, Google employees feel less like employees and more like entrepreneurs. The company is all about creativity and crazy ideas, and encourages their people to experiment and explore solutions to pressing problems. For instance, Gmail and Google News were conceived by engineers who are allowed to spend 20 percent of their work time on projects that aren't part of their job descriptions.

Despite having more than 10,000 employees worldwide, founders Larry Page and Sergey Brin will listen to suggestions and answer questions produced by employees. They know that to stay on top they will need new ideas—a lot of them. So the company has set up an easy-to-use internal system for Google employees to record ideas where they are safe, and where others in the companys can see and comment on them. Product managers regularly search the system for the best ideas, and the person who came up with it is put in charge of making it work. The bigger picture is Google's core belief that a good idea can come from anyone, anywhere in the company.

IBM

Competitive companies must change with the times. For anyone who has followed IBM throughout the years, you can clearly see they have been innovative and open to change, though not always at a rapid rate. Today, the company is open to creative collaboration and embracing employee ideas. When "Big Blue" launched its online idea-exchange program, it was with the intention of finding better ways to drive the company forward into the future.

Innovation Jam (as the program is called) allows a large number of participants, from clients and customers to employees and consultants, to exchange ideas electronically. More than 50,000 IBM employees "attended" a virtual conference with the goal of generating as many new ideas as possible. The company also uses collaborative tools and social networks to get the most from the best and brightest people. They then bring these ideas to life, build on them, test them, and take them to market using interactive Websites. (They have also put technical training on YouTube.)

IDEO

There are good ideas and then there are groundbreaking ones. It would be impossible to argue that the Apple mouse and the Palm V aren't two products that presented a profound change in how people interacted with technology. Silicon Valley-based Ideo had a hand in both products. The secret to their success is constant and consistent brainstorming sessions. Ideo believes that the best ideas come from collaboration and collection, and makes it a major part of its staff's day-to-day regimen—encouraging free thinking and wild ideas.

NIKE

At the footwear and apparel company's Tennessee location (responsible for distribution), it has enacted a program called ACT, which stands for Approaching Change Together. Teams are able to look at the workplace and suggest ideas for improvement online or during breakfasts with senior leaders. The company is also very good at recognizing employees for their contributions. The result is a corporate culture where ideas are welcome and appreciated.

NORDSTROM

The edict at the Seattle-based retail giant is, hire the best people and encourage them to use good judgment at all times. When it comes to good judgment, that means making sure the customer is always satisfied—and then some. All employers are empowered to solve problems and service customers without being micromanaged. For the salespeople, it's almost as though they are running their own businesses, which means they can be flexible with their approach to sales. Nordstrom's service is so extraordinary because employees have to come up with new and unique ways to exceed expectations. How they do it is by never saying no. This means they must discover creative ways to deliver on their promises, and collaborate to find new and improved ways to service their customers.

NORTHRUP GRUMMAN

On Northrup Grumman's Website under "Careers" the defense contractor invites potential employees to "Join us as we transform wild ideas, rough sketches, and stringent requirements into reality."

PEPSI

Pepsi Bottling Group has been very good at retaining its top talent in part because the company believes in fresh thinking and new ideas, and appreciating and recognizing the people that solve problems. The company looks for innovators and people with a strong entrepreneurial spirit who can work well as a team. The company's CEO, Eric Foss, worked his way up Pepsi's corporate ladder after being hired more than 25 years earlier. It's not surprising that his philosophy on innovation is that the best new ideas come from the people who have been at the company the longest. The key is to develop talent and show appreciation and recognition for their input and ideas.

PER SE *and* THE FRENCH LAUNDRY

Thomas Keller's ultra-luxe Per Se in New York and The French Laundry in Napa are often referred to as palaces of fine dining, and server training doesn't stray far from that royal allusion. To fine-tune the flow in the dining room, servers are given lessons in the minuet—an 18th-century ballroom dance. "First impressions are huge in our restaurants," says Keller's partner, Laura Cunningham. "A single movement or expression can greatly change someone's perception of the ambiance, so the staff is continually coached on body positioning and stance."

When Cunningham discovered the connection between the controlled movements of the minuet, which stresses graciousness and manners, and her ideal dining room "flow," she hired a baroque-style choreographer. At first staffers "thought we were a bit crazy," she admits. "But after the initial embarrassment of dancing with their coworkers, they appreciated what the teacher had to offer and all our servers took something from it."

SEIMENS

At this electronics manufacturing company, employees can not only come up with a great idea, but they can implement it too. These are ideas that can make a difference in the day-to-day in the life of an employee and are welcomed as part of the company's Program for the Achievement of Continuous Efficiency (PACE) ideation system. Ideas big and small from all levels of employees are recognized and rewarded.

SOUTHWEST AIRLINES

Southwest has embraced creativity through an unwavering belief in the power of people, playfulness, and individuality, and the result is a stronger bottom line.

"People are our most important asset," states Southwest's Website and other materials. The company is committed to its employees to the point of operating by highly creative, untraditional principles. First, employees aren't "human resources," they're people. What in any other company would be called the Human Resources Department is called the People Department. And since 1973, all Southwest employees are part owners of the company.

Southwest has always mixed creativity into its business. The people of Southwest have historically contributed creative ideas that lead to innovative changes.

STARBUCKS

What's your Starbucks idea? Revolutionary or simple, they want to hear it. That's the message you'll get when you go to their social-networking site, MyStarbucksIdea.com, where you can see and share ideas, as well as discuss and vote on them. "You know better than anyone else what you want from Starbucks," they remind us on the site. "So tell us. We're here, and we're ready to make ideas happen.... Together, we will shape the future of Starbucks. Your idea. Your Starbucks."

MyStarbucksIdea.com is their online community dedicated solely to idea generation and development. All submitted ideas are reviewed by Starbucks "Idea Partners"—employees who are experts in their respective fields. Additionally, the ideas are voted on by the public (once you're a registered member of the site). The most popular and most innovative ideas that are the best fit for Starbucks are then presented to key decision-makers for further consideration. And the best of the ideas can be followed on the site to see how they're being implemented.

TOYOTA

The highly successful Toyota Creative Ideas and Suggestion System (TCISS) operated by the Toyota Motors Corporation generated more than 20 million suggestions for improving manufacturing processes throughout a span of 40 years. The average number of suggestions submitted by each employee per year is close to 50, or one suggestion per employee per week. More than 95 percent of the workforce contributes suggestions; the most remarkable statistic from Toyota is that more than 90 percent of the suggestions are implemented. The basis of its success was the solid long-term commitment of *key managers* at Toyota. The system was introduced by Managing

Director Eiji Toyoda when it became clear during the post-WWII economic recovery that Toyota's production facilities needed to be modernized. Ironically, Toyoda got the idea from a Ford Motor Company plant he had visited in the summer of 1950.

TRADER JOE'S

Many of the companies profiled in this chapter rely on sophisticated systems to monitor innovative ideas. At Trader Joe's (a specialty grocery chain), they use a very simple system: They listen to their customers. You would guess this means via e-mail and phone or through focus groups, but, similar to many of the items they carry, their approach to feedback is more organic. Managers and employees are very close to their customers and listen when someone on the retail floor or at the cash register gives them feedback about a product or service. Then, these ideas are sent to buyers (people who buy wholesale for the chain) who may swap out a product, or to an appropriate manager who can make adjustments as needed.

TRAVELOCITY

When Travelocity found out from a poll that many of their customers (and even their own employees) would welcome a chance to change the world on their next vacation, the Southlake, Texas–based company came up with a plan to help people give back. They created $5,000 grants to help those who want to help others through "volunteer vacations."

TWO CHEFS

"I used to have a linen bill that was $1,400 a month," says Jan Jorgenson, owner of Two Chefs, a 100-seat restaurant in

South Miami, Florida. "A cook would go in and get 30 side towels for use during a shift; they'd keep on grabbing a fresh one. Side towels are expensive; 35 cents apiece." The same thing would happen with napkins. "Every time a waiter polished a glass they'd take a new napkin. That's 10 cents."

Solution? Put one employee in charge of the linens, and provide a cash incentive for keeping costs down. "I said, 'I'd like my linen bill to be $1,000. You manage it, and whatever it comes in under that, you get to keep.'" Now, one waiter keeps the linens under lock and key and doles out supplies daily: aprons, towels, tablecloths, and napkins. The monthly bill is about $600 to $700 now. "It's like he's managing his own business," says Jorgenson, "and I'm saving on my bill."

WESTINGHOUSE

At Westinghouse Electronic Systems, suggestions to save money are taken seriously. Employees who share their ideas are rewarded by seeing some of their suggestions implemented immediately—and with a cash prize based on how much money the company saved or on the merit of the idea. These ideas have ranged from a $100 method for securing computers with sensitive information (versus the old $10,000 method), to switching the filters in its rooftop air-handling units on 30 of its buildings, thus saving the company $48,000 in the first year alone.

WHIRLPOOL

When Whirlpool's Chairman and CEO wanted the appliance-maker to be the best in the business at innovation, the company turned to its own employees. They responded by brainstorming wild ideas, many of which went on to become a reality.

Employees are encouraged to submit ideas on the company's intranet site, and has a team to find the best suggestions and get them to the next step.

Appendix
Ready, Set, Go

Held in the palms of thousands of disgruntled people over the centuries have been ideas worth millions—if they only had taken the first step and then followed through.
—Robert M. Hayes

WILD IDEA CLUB (N) — A collaborative system to solve workplace problems, improve efficiency, and boost your bottom line.

The Wild Idea Club concept works best when everyone's ideas can be heard without judgment—and then recorded, discussed, expanded upon by others, and honed until they can be pitched to the decision-makers and ultimately used for the betterment of the business. The people who presented the ideas are then acknowledged or rewarded in some way.

You can and should start a Wild Idea Club.

As you have read in the examples in this book, employees want to share their ideas and solve problems. They just need a safe way to do it—and feel as though their input matters. It's not that complicated. This is good news for managers. If managers will give their teams a little time, a reasonable amount of resources, and a small amount of direction, a Wild Idea Club will thrive. They need the time and place to meet, a specific challenge to tackle, and maybe most important of all, a manager who will listen to and implement their best suggestions. That's it in a nutshell. The only catch is, we are dealing with all kinds of different people and personalities. So we will lay out all the ways to make it work in this section—because we want you to reap the rewards a club such as this will produce.

One of the biggest benefits of a club is the ability to take a good idea and build on it to make it a *great* one. This happens when a group of people can add their own ideas to the original concept and all share in the credit. When members of a club are allowed to freely blend their ideas with others, without the worry of being ridiculed and reprimanded (or failing to be recognized or rewarded), they will feel open to share the best they have to offer—and everyone wins. Here's how to make it happen, step by step.

STEP 1: THE RIGHT STUFF

The Right Mindset

The process begins with a forward-thinking manager, executive, or staff person who is willing to tap into the collective creativity and genius of his or her staff. A manager with the right mindset realizes good ideas can come from anyone at any level in the company—and even outside the business, such as customers, vendors, distributors, and other partners. This makes sense when you consider that those in the trenches usually have more contact with customers and a better understanding of the day-to-day details than those higher up the corporate ladder. The right mindset also means managers must commit to a belief that all ideas are potentially good ideas at first, and sometimes wild ones, when worked through, are the genesis of truly workable solutions to pressing problems.

It's not enough to say "we welcome new ideas"; managers must make a concerted effort to not pass judgment until after a pitch, and then use their own expertise, experience, and executive influence to guide the group to develop the proposal to a point at which a crazy idea actually makes sense. Give the group guidelines and guidance. When members of the club have the freedom to brainstorm plus the parameters to keep things focused, managers get the most usable ideas in the least amount of time.

A manager with the right mindset will also ask the group to go wild with ideas, but to only bring forward their best, and, when possible, pitch them with a proposal or plan for implementation. In addition, the manager's job is to keep an open mind when it comes to creative solutions, and to also open the minds of the club members, to help them see the business side and bottom line of what they propose. When these two intersect (the ideas are innovative and in step with the company's goals), you have a winning formula.

However, not all ideas can or should be judged on the simple potential for them to make or save money. Sometimes things that improve the corporate culture and create an improved work

environment pay off too. But even those solutions and suggestions influence the bottom line through increased employee
retention, improved productivity, and enhancing the image or
brand of the business.

The Right People

Of course you want the best and brightest people included
in the club, but you don't gauge people's qualifications solely
by their job titles or how many degrees they hold. (And a
person's pecking order in the company hierarchy is not relevant in the meetings.) You want people who excel at their
jobs, whether they spend more time in the boardroom or clean-
ing the bathrooms. You also want key people who have a track
record of coming up with ideas and knowing how to develop
them.

You want people who care about the company. How will
you know who they are? When you announce you are starting
a Wild Idea Club that seeks suggestions from employees to
improve the company and the workplace, these will be the first
people to volunteer.

The Right Reason

Wild Ideas Clubs can be started to solve a specific problem
or improve a project; they can be developed around a department, or just as a way to capture ideas and give employees an
outlet for their frustrations. From our perspective, there is no
reason *not* to start one. If you are interested in increasing productivity, production, and sales, do it. If you want to cut costs
and complaints, do it. If you want to make your people feel
important and improve their morale, do it. If you want to make
your life easier as a manager, do it. Just do it.

The Right Time

There really is no right or wrong time to start a Wild Idea Club, because any time you start one is a good time. However, a club that starts at a time when you and the company need specific solutions tends to produce the most tangible results. When times get tough and you need to get more done with fewer people and resources, this is the time to start one. And if the company (or your department) simply isn't where you want it to be, start one.

Basically, the best day to start a Wild Idea Club is any day that ends with a "y." We're only half kidding, because there are advantages to each specific day of the week. For example, a club that meets on the first Friday of the month in the afternoon will be much more efficient (people tend to cut to the chase when the weekend looms large). Mondays are good because it sets the tone for the week. Wednesdays work well because people should be caught up for the week (stop laughing) and can brainstorm with a clear head. More important than the when, the goal is to have regular meetings and real issues.

The Right Place

If time or cost is an issue, finding a quiet place on the premises makes sense. If that won't spark enough innovative thought—the meeting rooms are too small or drab, or lack whiteboards and other ways to capture ideas—then by all means take the meetings elsewhere. We have heard of Wild Idea Clubs meeting in private rooms in restaurants, libraries, and even vacant classrooms. Meeting outdoors can be inspiring; so can meeting in the specific place where the problem persists. But the best meeting places have Internet access, comfortable seating, a surface to write on, and, perhaps most important of all, as few distractions as possible. Hmm...maybe that drab, window-less meeting space will work after all.

The Right Resources

The items most requested at Wild Idea Club meetings include something to eat, something to drink, and something to write with and on (usually in that order). More important than having these items is a big board or wall to post ideas in progress for all to see. We prefer using those giant Post-it notes (the flip-chart-sized ones) because they stick to almost anything, are easily seen from around a room, and can be organized and reorganized easily.

We all know children are more open-minded and creative than their adult counterparts. Because we all had that kid-like quality at one time or another, it makes sense to have what seems like silly things on hand to encourage creativity—everything from clay to crayons. The main point is to have immediately available the items necessary to encourage and foster creative thinking, to develop ideas, and to capture them.

The Right Incentives

The difference between an employee who feels powerless and one who is empowered is enormous. The person who feels he or she is "just an employee" will respond accordingly by doing just enough to keep his or her job by "going through the motions." Whether or not the company does well isn't this employee's concern. On the other hand, a person participating in a Wild Idea Club, in which one's ideas and insights are valued, is much more committed to making a difference in the organization. When you add in recognition and rewards for the best ideas implemented, you get a whole other level of commitment to the company. It's amazing what employees will do for a simple pat on the back, a piece about them in the company newsletter, or pizza for their whole team. Awards and rewards are the spark that can fuel the creativity of your people, and ultimately make your job easier.

STEP 2: CHOOSING WILD IDEA CLUB MEMBERS

The ideal number of people in a club is 12 to 20 members. (If it gets too big, it can be broken up into teams, or another club can be formed. In fact, you can have several clubs within a company, depending how large it is.) But who do we include? We know that everyone has ideas, many of them excellent, at all levels of a company. The key is to have a broad representation of perspectives on the issues at hand, the company, and potential solutions.

Time of service is not a concern. The longtime employee has great insights, and so does the newbie. Longtimers usually understand things better, and their experience is invaluable when brainstorming. However, the naïveté of the newbies is important in the process as well. They have no prior knowledge of what works or doesn't work and can come at the problem from a new perspective—one of possibilities.

The advantage in including people from different levels and departments in the company is not only the different perspectives, but also how quickly you can determine the viability of something due to the various knowledge bases. Plus, after a meeting in which a breakthrough idea is put forward, the members can go back to their bosses in the different departments to get the help needed to champion something along through proper channels and cut the red tape.

Sure, there are people who will make ideal members to a Wild Idea Club, but that doesn't mean they should be the only ones included. Part of the Wild Idea Club process is sifting through the many ideas generated to get to the best by putting them to the test. In addition to the creative, innovative, supportive, and positive people, having a naysayer on board provides balance. (It only takes one person who is highly skeptical, overly logical, and way too uptight to balance out a group of 10 to 12 innovative thinkers.) Because they see problems where others don't, they're valuable in shooting holes in ideas and anticipating objections *before* a decision-maker does during a formal pitch.

Likewise, whereas complainers and whiners would not instantly come to mind as good mastermind partners, if their complaints center on making the company more competitive and a better place to work, a Wild Idea Club could be just what they need—and why you need them. People who have the company's best interests at heart, no matter how misdirected they may have been in the past, could be a perfect fit for the club when they become emboldened, empowered, entrepreneurial, and engaged by new ideas. Then, they are not just employees, but partners.

Eventually, an idea has to be carried forward, and for this you need a few members who have good presentation or sales skills. These people will need to sell an idea and the plan that goes with it to the decision-makers. A good presenter doesn't need any formal training; sometimes the best "salesperson" is the one who is most passionate about the idea (and maybe even the one who came up with it in the first place). In addition to a person who can pitch, it's good to have at least one person who knows how to plan. This likely left-brained, rational person will help guide the group when the time comes to sift through the ideas and find the gold. Finally, although the facilitator role can be rotated, the skill set that makes for an ideal leader includes patience, open-mindedness, time-management ability, authoritativeness, and, of course, exceptional people skills.

This leads to the importance of having different thinking styles. Having a room full of right-brained idea types can lead to amazing leaps of insights and big-picture problem-solving, but right-brainers are also the pie-in-the-sky people with their heads in the clouds looking at the big picture. Conversely, left-brainers are at their best when using their logic and practicality to break ideas down into a manageable series of steps. But they can get bogged down in details. By including people with both brain types and encouraging them to use their strengths, you get the best of both worlds. Here are some further suggestions about who to include and how to get the most out of them.

- One company had people switch positions for a day so the administrative people could see how difficult the executive positions were, and the executives went out on sales calls and worked in the field. When they held their Wild Idea Club meetings afterward, there was a much better understanding of what work was like for all involved, from the mail room up to the board room.

- If possible (and if it doesn't violate any confidentiality agreements), allow guests into your club from an entirely different industry and walk of life to see what they come up with. They have no preconceived notions and offer a fresh perspective.

- An ad agency incorporated members' kids into a meeting when faced with a unique problem for which they simply couldn't come up with a solution. The children were the primary problem-solvers for the meeting, and, lo and behold, one of them came up with the idea that ultimately solved the issue.

💡 Have various leader types attend your meetings—a local rabbi or priest, a grizzled industry veteran who knows everything but is no longer actively working, a professional speaker or facilitator, or whomever is your version of Yoda.

Is there anyone who *shouldn't* be a part of the meetings? Probably not, but just a word of caution: When an owner, CEO, or even a manager is present, it can be a distraction and inhibit innovative ideas. At least some people won't share those ideas for fear of looking silly and possibly losing respect or their jobs.

STEP 3: WHEN AND WHERE TO HOST THE MEETINGS

When

It's rather ironic that most highly creative people are not morning people, because the early hours are best for most people to meet. When it comes to choosing a time for a Wild Idea Club meeting, there is magic in the morning. A morning meeting can also mean fewer distractions, which tend to creep up throughout the day.

Many clubs meet during the lunch hour, because most meetings should be short and sweet: An hour or two is ideal;

any more is pushing it. It's amazing how much energy there is during the first hour and how quickly it can drop off after that.

If the club can't meet often, and longer sessions are required, giving short but frequent breaks works well. Fewer but longer breaks would seem to make sense, but members tend to disappear to check their e-mail, make calls, take care of a couple of tasks, and ultimately not be thinking of the problem at hand (or worse, not return). The best breaks keep people close and allow them to stretch their legs and minds by continuing to talk about things in the meeting, but in sub groups or one-on-one.

If you can eliminate the reasons people would want to leave by having everything handy—food, drink, and Internet access—they will tend to hang around. This is especially true if you need to hold a super session (one that lasts all day). There have also been Wild Idea Club retreats such that a team gets away and is totally immersed in solving a problem or seeking several new ideas to benefit the business. The dynamics are a little different, because you can't keep people cooped up for days. But getting out in a different environment (or nature) and mixing in idea-inspiring games works really well. It's also an interesting dynamic in which members who meet socially after an intensive session often have that "aha!" idea. Bottom line: all work and no play can stifle innovative thought.

We discussed the best days for a meeting earlier, but it's worth noting again that there isn't a "bad" day to get a group together. However, the best days may be midweek, in case people have a case of "the Mondays" or put it out of their minds over the weekend and end up missing the meeting. Likewise, when guests attend meetings, midweek works well.

Lastly, keep in mind that full-day sessions usually require another full day (or at least half a day) beforehand to get everything set up and organized. Then, allow at least a half-day following the session to debrief and pack everything up.

Where

Many people prefer to hold their Wild Idea Club meetings off site for a variety of reasons, including the need to get away from work and everyday responsibilities. Another reason to move a meeting away from the office is that innovative thinking can be enhanced by the environment in which you meet. These venues can be as "out there" as a bowling alley, a train, or the beach. But when all is said and done, the best location is simply one where people have a place to sit, paper can be affixed to a wall, Internet access is free and easy, there are electrical outlets, there are no distractions, food and drink can be consumed, and, of course, bathrooms are close by. That's not to say you can't move meetings around to keep it fresh—you should, even if all the elements that make a place perfect aren't there.

Meetings can be held on site, but when the budget allows, moving them to another location (hotel, conference facility, restaurant) can be best for longer sessions with a lot of members (many of whom may be from out of town). If you can't afford the time or expense to rent a room, it helps to make the normal meeting place look less like a conference room and more like a space where wild ideas would be welcomed. You could decorate the walls, remove all the chairs, cover the walls with paper, or bring in art supplies and toys to the meeting. The good thing about doing it in a controlled space is the privacy: no distractions, and your ideas won't be overheard. However, if you can use a vacant space (before or after hours, or off season) that is quiet and private, with room to move, and where there is Internet access, this opens up a lot of possibilities (a museum, yoga studio, vacant art gallery, or an empty classroom, to name a few).

Lastly, we've mentioned Internet access a few times, so it's worth pointing out that this isn't just a nicety or a symptom of online addiction; it's practical for meetings so things can be looked up immediately as necessary, without someone having to "get back to" the club on the issue. Often, the "get back to" part never happens by the next meeting.

Virtual Meetings

Keep in mind that having a "meeting" doesn't always mean the attendees are all in the same room. In fact, none of them may be. Using social-networking tools such as Facebook, MySpace, LinkedIn, or Twitter to set up and run a Wild Idea Club lets you tap in to the ideas of people throughout the company, and even throughout the world.

If you don't already have a system in place to communicate with other offices, a number of companies can set up a temporary virtual meeting space. A wide range of mainstream companies offer online communications and collaboration tools, such as WebEx, Citrix, Microsoft, and IBM. Video conferencing has come a long way, and is excellent for communicating and collaborating, but its drawback is expense. These video-conferencing systems—which include several specialized screens and enhanced acoustics—can be supplied by companies such as Cisco, HP, and Polyco. Or, of course, virtual meetings can be done simply using e-mail, blogs, or message boards. As you'll see later in this chapter, Google even provides a tool that can be very effective for online collaboration.

Virtual meetings not only save travel time and expense, but, depending on how they are run, also allow people to participate without losing productivity. Ideas will be bandied about, and employees get to know one another better and forge relationships based on common ground. They now have a better grasp of what distant coworkers look like and what their job responsibilities are. Plus, younger workers prefer this type of online interaction, and it could increase their productivity and creativity at the same time. Lastly, the introverts in the group will find this format more comfortable for sharing their ideas and insights.

Regardless of the technology, the key is still the same as with any meetings: Focus on something specific, and gather as many ideas as possible before deciding what's worthy and what's not.

The Playroom Concept

Many of the most creative companies (advertising and marketing agencies, tech companies, and other forward-thinking businesses) have a creativity center. Here you will find everything from art supplies and games to toys and sporting gear. There is a method to this madness; many times the best ideas come from goofing off and playing around. As counterproductive as this sounds, having a place where your people can play and hang out can help them help the company by brainstorming between meetings, without the pressure to produce anything.

STEP 4: PRE-MEETING CHECKLIST

Research

Research is to the innovative process what stretching is to a runner: It's the perfect place to start. You can learn a lot about what will work when you first find what's out there. Survey coworkers, read your trade journal, talk to customers, and go online. Many times a little of this pre-meeting homework will speed up the process. To help with this, give participants a clear understanding of the focus of the meeting and/or detail the problem you want to solve.

Materials

As mentioned before, make sure all the necessary things are already in the room before the meeting starts, so there is no excuse or reason to leave. Items that can aid in the Wild Idea Club process include digital and video cameras, laptop computer with wi-fi, blank notepads, paper in all sizes and colors, blank flipchart pads, index cards, copy paper, magazines on a variety of subjects, a timer (for the facilitator), name tags, colored markers in various thicknesses, pens, scissors, chalk, games and toys, cardboard, stickers, tape, glue sticks, masking tape, unusual items (bubbles, feather boas, etch-a-sketches, hula hoops), and musical instruments. In addition, include some crayons, silly putty, blocks, foam, fabric, paints, glitter, sequins, and other craft supplies so that people can *show* what they mean. Remember, the visual side of the brain is the side that fosters innovation. Give every member an idea notebook or binder with pockets so they can keep and save their ideas, jot notes, or rip out and store relevant articles. If you are in a product-related business, it helps to bring in a variety of your products and packaging forms to have on display.

Lastly, spend a little money to have some prizes to award throughout the sessions. They can be as simple and inexpensive as candy bars. You can go a long way toward participation (and idea proliferation) with a little incentive.

Environment

The amount of time and expense you put into creating the environment will depend upon the length and focus of the meeting. Decorate with anything colorful, such as balloons, flowers, art, and sculptures. It is highly recommended that the environment be filled with as much creative stimuli as possible, yet allow room for ideas to germinate and be displayed. Some businesses already have "creative" rooms that are painted with bright colors and have interesting art on the walls; these are ideal.

Make sure the tables are set for small groups, and whenever possible, use round tables to foster mutual sharing and collaboration. For similar benefits when using rectangular tables, arrange two of them side by side to form a square. Alternately, odd-shaped tables can be good for creating a unique and inspiring setting.

A key component of the environment is food and drink. Aside from addressing hunger, eating and drinking are very primitive-based human bonding activities. And both activities tend to spur people to communicate more, which is obviously great for collaborative purposes.

Not just any food and drink is ideal, however. Make sure whoever handles these knows to not just get sugary foods that tend to be office staples—donuts, pastries, cookies. Although it may be more expensive, include healthy options so everyone's minds functions at their best. Not necessarily healthy, but proven to accelerate mental activity, caffeine is a smart ingredient to have on hand in one or another of its forms. And lastly, fun food items and packaging can stimulate creative thought as well. If you're at a loss for what these can be, just check out the kids' displays and shelves at the grocery stores.

STEP 5: THE FACILITATOR'S ROLE

The facilitator is the most important person at a Wild Idea Club meeting. If this person allows the meeting to get too wild, ideas won't come out of it. On the other hand, if it's run the way a country club is (too uptight), it won't work either. Ideas need to be allowed to come to light and be captured, built on, and then moved forward to the next step. The facilitator has to do this strategically, carefully, and thoughtfully, while managing the topic, time, and people. But this role also includes giving the group permission to have fun—injecting humor, encouraging silliness, and allowing playfulness.

Another goal and function of the facilitator is to redirect and keep everyone's focus on discovering solutions. In doing so, he or she establishes guidelines, sets the ground rules, and occasionally breaks them if it will ultimately serve the purpose of the group. As meetings progress, the facilitator is also responsible for delegating the next steps by aligning people's strengths with necessary follow-through tasks. And during meetings, he or she works in tandem with a "scribe/recorder" so the facilitator can be more engaged in listening and leading during the process.

Good facilitators realize that everyone has a different way of learning and interacting. Some are auditory, many are tactile, most are visual, and still more are emotional. Facilitators should try to blend these in, incorporating all senses when possible.

To keep the ball rolling while trying to come up with an idea, they should continue asking questions such as "Why not...?" or "What if...?" or "How about...?" When asking the group a question, allow a few minutes of silence to give the introverts time to gather their thoughts—it's not uncommon for extroverts to begin speaking immediately, and this can cause the introverts to withdraw and not speak up.

Lastly, good meeting facilitators don't let things get too far off track. Though brainstorming should be nonlinear, for the purposes of problem-solving, stay focused on the topic at hand.

To help ensure this, clearly define the issue being brainstormed first. Then, to protect against other ideas being lost, if one comes up that's not related to the issue being discussed, record it anyhow, but note that it is off topic. You can always come back to it later or when relevant.

STEP 6: SETTING THE GROUND RULES

When it comes to creativity, rules are made to be broken. When it comes to a brainstorming session, a few rules can keep your Wild Idea Club from becoming just a wild club—there is a difference. As strange as it sounds, having some parameters to keep everyone focused, as well as some guidelines to go by, will always end up making the group more creative.

The most important rule of all is to never be negative about an idea, especially early in the process. If members critique ideas in the first phase of a Wild Idea Club session, it could stunt the growth of a good idea and prevent others from sharing theirs. The wilder the idea, the better; you can always go back and figure out what *wouldn't* work. Unlimited thinking is the key. Although this may seem obvious, it needs emphasizing: Nothing good comes from negativity early in the ideation process.

If only we could shut our left brains down for a while (the critical, analytical side) so our more creative right brains could run free, we'd all be more innovative, right? Well, amazingly, you can. By having something tedious or repetitious for people to do while brainstorming (walking works well), their left brains are kept busy. To further curb premature criticism, you must have a rule that no negativity is allowed during the ideation process. Here are some other good ground rules.

♥ Eliminate distractions in meetings. Make your "no phones or BlackBerrys" policy a zero-tolerance one. Avoid meeting places where there are background distractions, such as a window with a lot of activity outside.

💡 Reward, but not simply for a "best idea." There can be a competitive aspect added to a Wild Idea Club meeting, but it shouldn't just be for the best idea, especially if the same person keeps coming up with them.

💡 Encourage humor. It is a great tool at Wild Idea Club meetings, so, as long as no one is getting hurt or it doesn't get ugly, embrace it.

💡 Only allow one person to talk at a time.

💡 Establish as few rules as possible, with these primarily being ones that help members respect one another and each others' ideas.

Finally, remember that rules are made to be broken. What we mean here is that companies, especially those that have been around for a while, often have a pile of rules in place. Obviously, most of these are probably for good reason. But sometimes, employees will subconsciously (or consciously) squash an idea that has potential because they know it would break some company rule. Maybe the rule needs to be broken, changed, or eliminated for the benefits the idea will bring. So, for the sake of seeking all possibilities, start off by imagining there are no existing company policies and procedures. Make it seem as if any idea could become a reality regardless of the company's current restrictions.

STEP 7: IDENTIFYING THE PROBLEM

The Wild Idea Club concept works best with specific problems. The better defined they are, the better the results. It's an incredible thing to watch when everyone in the club "gets it"—that they are working on innovative ways of improving something, and are so clear about what needs to be done they are almost falling over one another with ideas. It happens. But it only happens when someone (the manager or the facilitator) has an understanding of what needs fixing and/or what it will look like when it is fixed. That means making it manageable, quantifiable, desirable, and, maybe most important of all, viable.

This should begin with a good description of what's wrong or by explaining what something will look like when it's right. Better yet, when a group can truly *see* a sample of what they are aiming for (how a competitor did it or a company in another industry made it happen), that really gets people's engines going at full speed. One of the best techniques to get answers to perplexing problems is to ask compelling questions. These questions can range from "What if we...?" to "Why don't we...?" and everything in between. When you ask the right question you have the potential to get the perfect answer. Think about all the combinations of questions you can come up with just starting with the words *who, what, why, where, when, how, how much,* and *how many.* It's almost limitless. The best questions are usually not fuzzy ones, though. If you ask vague questions, you'll get vague answers. "How can we improve our department to increase productivity next year by 20 percent?" is much better than "How can we make our department more productive?" It's not easy, because you want to be broad to encourage a wide array of solutions, but by being *too* broad you can lack the focus needed to solve something specific. On the other hand, if the focus is too narrow, you lose some of the creativity. For example, a question that might be too broad would be, "What can we do to make the office look better?" One that is too narrow might sound like, "What artwork can we put up to make the office look better?" As another example, you could probably devote an entire Wild Idea Club meeting to just exploring various ways everyone can do their jobs a little bit better. By asking everyone if there is a better way to do something *specific*, you may be surprised at the many different ways people can do their jobs more effectively and efficiently.

Have people experience the problem before solving it. For example, if there is a way to become the customer for a day, do it. Instead of hiring mystery shoppers, have various employees take on the task. By changing everyone's perspective and involving all senses in the creative process (through immersion), members will have many more ideas percolating in their minds.

Chances are someone else has solved your problem. One Wild Idea Club meeting could be used just to do research. Find out more by learning about your counterpart in a different part of the country, learning about a different department or corporation, reviewing your competitor's Website (or possibly take a field trip to their business), or using a search engine to see where it takes you.

When first starting a club, one thing to watch out for is beginning with a controversial or emotional issue. If one needs to be solved (for example, some form of inequity in the workplace), make it the topic of a later meeting. Better to let the Wild Idea Club form and bond over a more innocuous, easy-to-solve problem or two before tackling tougher ones.

Lastly, remember that nearly all big problems are solved with a series of smaller solutions. Instead of having members struggle to come up with one way to deal with a gigantic issue (and likely get frustrated and discouraged), make it more manageable by breaking it down to the point where it's practical and easier to tackle each step.

STEP 8: GENERATING IDEAS

The word *idea* is just one of the three in "Wild Idea Club," but it is clearly the most important. The word *wild* is important too, because the best ideas may been seen as wild at first, but when run through the filter of the people and process of the club they can become rational, practical, usable solutions. But it all begins with ideas—lots of them—and then the members of the club add to, adjust, and eventually promote the best ones. A Wild Idea Club may end up being a place where people socialize, network, and build bonds (all tangential benefits for everyone and the company), but first and foremost it is a format for harvesting and developing ideas.

There are as many ways to start the process of getting to good ideas as there are ideas, but it always begins with this premise: There are no bad ideas...to start. One way to make sure people go for quantity instead of quality with their suggestions is to set a number of ideas to shoot for. You don't want everyone stop as soon as they hear what seems like a good idea when the *great* one is still out there. When you aim for 77 ideas, for example, it helps people open up, because they aren't expected to hit the big idea to begin with. Plus, numbering your ideas makes them much easier to track and refer to.

Another common creativity killer for members of the club is thinking too far ahead in the beginning. Don't let people get hung up on the implementation of an idea (and whether it will work or not, or ever be used) before they finish flushing out all the possibilities. And be on the lookout for people who become too attached to an idea, so much so that they've lost the ability to let it go, if necessary, or see it from another perspective. There is often more than one right answer. Again, if you stop when you get to a good solution, you may be missing the great one just around the corner. The smartest people in the world don't nail the problem on their first try. In fact, the common thread that runs through big thinkers is they try and fail many, many times before getting big ideas right. Invariably, you will need to sift through numerous potential solutions before discovering the ultimate one. And it's not uncommon for the best idea to evolve out of lesser ones.

The creative part of the brain is a lot like a muscle (and for many it can be a little flabby), so it needs to be warmed up and stretched. This is ideally done by starting Wild Idea Club meetings not by rushing into whatever is the topic of the day, but by getting everyone going on something else. For example:

💡 Ask an unrelated question, such as "What was the funniest thing that happened to you yesterday?" Humor fosters creativity, so this question is a good way to relax everyone, brighten up the day, and open the mind to innovation. For bonus points (and extra creativity), have each person who responds describe how the funny moment could've been even funnier. Just start discussing a problem—again, not related to the main purpose of that day's meeting—with no preconceived notions and see what happens. Immerse yourself in it and see it from all angles. Often, an unrelated problem is best, because no one has any investment in the results or issue. One interesting example was a club that opened by coming up with what they envisioned would be a popular new food item at McDonald's. Although it wasn't a problem, per se, it gave them a simple and fun challenge to solve. And to keep anyone from overthinking the issue, the whole matter had to be tackled in five minutes. (The winning answer, by the way, was a giant soft pretzel shaped like the McDonald's arches.)

💡 Begin each meeting by varying the size of the subgroups—if you have 12 to 20 people, change it up by having everyone work in pairs, triads, or groups of five or six people.

Once a meeting gets going, the idea-generating process shouldn't stop, for whatever the duration of the meeting. Here are some ways to foster innovation and creativity in a Wild Idea Club setting, and proliferate ideas.

💡 Look for metaphors and communicate with them when appropriate. When Forrest Gump said, "Life is like a box of chocolates; you never know what you're gonna get," didn't you get a clear picture in your mind of that box of chocolates? Similes work too.

💡 List-making is very left-brained and linear. Instead, give people a stack of magazines and tell them to look for a solution visually, which is a function of the right brain (the side that fosters innovation).

💡 Online brainstorming can be like the TV game show *Who Wants to Be a Millionaire?* A person can use "lifelines" to phone a friend, do a quick Google search, or other "reaching out" ways to find solutions.

💡 One company started an idea board in the break room. It was a simple dry-erase board with a problem written in the middle. Anyone walking by was able to write in a solution around it (anony-mously). So, a Wild Idea Club can take many forms; consider what will work best for the situation, your workplace, and its members. A simple arrangement like that dry-erase board may be better and more productive than a more elaborate arrangement that ultimately falls apart because it's too time-consuming or cumbersome. The only "right" way to struc-ture your Wild Idea Club is the way that leads to the most participation and innovation.

💡 Similar to the previous example, employees at Hewlett Packard were asked to leave projects in progress out on their desks so another person could walk by and jot a suggestion or two on a pad of paper on top of the pile or file.

💡 To get really wild ideas, take a unique approach to anything and everything. Start the meeting at 11:11 instead of 11:00. Do a backwards meeting in which you start with the end in mind. Ask mem-bers who play music to bring in their instruments and incorporate them into their participation; those who sing would sing their input. Have a roundtable brainstorming sequence in which each person has to add to the previous person's suggestion—and make it rhyme. Have a costumed meeting, even if it's not Halloween. Or better yet, do a themed costume meeting—such as everyone dressing as a police officer and have donuts. We haven't heard of any club incorporating a food fight into a meet-ing, but that would be fun.

💡 Other meeting themes could be situational: "If I ran this company, I would…" "What would a 4-year-old do?" "What would my dad or mom do?" "What would Jesus do?" "What would Jimmy Buffett do?" These help stimulate ideas and give people a sense of ownership.

💡 Prototypes, role-playing, and proposals all help people visualize what the problem is or what the solution could look like and be like. Remember, the more senses you engage, the more sensible the ultimate solution will be.

💡 Having a box full of games, toys, and arts and crafts things may seem juvenile, but these can be the key to unlocking everyone's innovation. Get people to use their hands in the process—motor skills help thinking skills. It's no coincidence we engaged in these activities at the beginning of our schooling. But somehow they got pushed aside along the way. We started out writing and drawing with a box of 64 colored crayons, and now we're working day to day with a black pen and yellow highlighter—what happened?

💡 Begin by describing what work will be like after you have solved the problem. See if there are clues hidden in there.

💡 Think in paradoxes and opposites to stretch your ideas. For example, if the issue is a problematic copier in the office that there's no current budget to replace, brainstorm what you'd do if you had no copier.

- Try free-writing, in which people just riff or ramble on paper about the problem at hand. Free association is the verbal equivalent, such that people say whatever comes to mind about a problem; not necessarily looking for the solution, but just to make connections and associations.

- Do something out of your comfort zone—dance, improvisational acting, or yoga stretches.

- Go on shopping excursions—look for unusual items in unlikely places.

- Write a feature article or come up with a TV show about your idea.

- Pretend you are another (well-known) company, such as FedEx, Disney, or Google—how do you think they would solve your problem?

- Utilize the graphic technique called "mind mapping," in which the issue or problem is written and/or drawn in the center of a large paper, and then ideas are written and drawn around it with connections made between relevant items. It looks like a family tree gone crazy, but it harnesses the full range of mental skills—words, images, numbers, logic, rhythm, color, and spatial awareness—in a single, uniquely productive way.

- Don't be afraid to allow people to doodle, scribble, and write on the walls (assuming it's on paper or a white board). Ultimately, you want to make everything as fun as possible.

- Many times we stop brainstorming too soon. Before all ideas are reviewed and reconsidered, take the process to extremes by encouraging the most outlandish ideas possible, as a way to get the best ones. Even if the idea seems silly at first, you never know if something useful may come from it later on. Seemingly insane ideas are often discarded too early, so instead, see if something can be applied now or leads on a tangent to a different, more feasible idea. Give your ideas the path of least resistance.

💡 Lastly, don't forget about having members generating ideas on their own. Although being together leads to many potential solutions, working alone to solve a problem can also be efficient and effective. There are fewer distractions, inhibitions, and other group dynamics to deal with. Brainstorming solo and connecting electronically when someone needs advice, feedback, or just plain old interaction can be the best of both worlds. One way to do this is to get an idea (in writing) as far as one member can, and then send it to the group and see if they can build on it. An especially creative and effective technique is to write the problem and solution as a story, such as, "Once upon a time at my company..."—one person starts, writing perhaps a page, and then passes the story to the next person to build on. Everyone is encouraged to get wacky in contributing to the story. The goal is not to create a great piece of literature, but rather to create a vision of how the company can work through the particular problem that's the focus of the story.

STEP 9: CAPTURING YOUR IDEAS

Trust us, it's far more frustrating to have had a wonderful, stupendous, incredible idea and lose it than to have never had it at all. Ideas are easily lost if they are not captured in some way. The club *must* have a scribe (someone who makes sure ideas are either written, recorded, or both) at every meeting. This is the second-most important position, after the facilitator. It is also necessary to keep *all* ideas without passing judgment. Just get them down on something or somewhere safe—written, drawn, doodled, and/or recorded using audio or video. The scribe needs to document each and every idea, even if it seems impossible. Many people don't realize there are whiteboards that translate scribbles and examples into a form that can be downloaded directly to a computer. (Can't afford one? Hmm...sounds like a problem for a Wild Idea Club to solve.) There are many other ways of idea-catching and innovation-cultivating; some are old-school (flip charts and index cards) and some are more modern (laptops, networking, e-mail).

Many people have the impression that a Wild Idea Club meeting (or the like) is just people shouting their ideas at the top of their lungs with a person jotting them all down on a flip chart. Sure, that does happen, but another way to capture ideas is to have people write down their own. A great way to do this is with large Post-It notes, and then the ideas can be passed around or put up for all to see. These same ideas can then be organized, categorized, criticized (if need be), and finally put into a form that shows the solutions are clear. Another form of this collaboration is for your solution to be written on a piece of paper and passed to the person next to you for his or her contribution. The paper is then passed to another person until it's made its way around the room. One benefit of this is that it allows the quiet people to put in their two "senses" worth.

Lastly, the old suggestion box still works, as long as someone works *it* and there's not a paper shredder hiding inside. But the "new school" version is even better because it's easy and everyone can see it: social-networking sites and brainstorming tools. These are so useful because they bring employees together and provide a format and forum to share information and bounce ideas back and forth, without having to leave one's desk. Plus, they're ideal for smaller companies that can't afford the expensive collaboration software applications. And though it's not a social-networking site in the "traditional" sense of the term, Google Docs (*www.google.com/docs*) is another excellent collaborative tool that allows anyone with a Google account to create and post documents online. Forgive us, Microsoft, but it's like having Office online for all to use and share. Plus, the program has user privileges (checking documents in and out), multi-user creation (two or more people can work on the same document at once, with a record of who wrote what), and versioning (a history of each document). So, it only takes a little imagination to see how this can be used for online collaboration between members across an office, across the country, or across the world. Oh, and as with most Google tools, it's completely free.

STEP 10: SELECTING YOUR BEST IDEAS

We have already established there are no bad ideas (in the beginning), but of course, some are better than others, and then there are the best ones, and finally, the big one. But how do you get to the point at which it's clear which ideas are going to make the cut, which ones won't, and which *one* to run with? Ultimately, the criteria will depend on the many factors that are unique to your situation, but these suggestions should help you examine, evaluate, and endorse the right one (for your company).

- ♀ Ask people to rate the ideas based on their first reaction—their intuitive response—to get a true right-brain reading. Later, you can take a left-brain (logical and linear) approach to highlight and determine the keepers.

- ♀ Have a cooling-off period to wait on selecting the best ideas. This could be a break between brainstorming and choosing favorite suggestions, or it could be the next meeting when ideas are evaluated. Regardless of the timing, it's always a help to put the collected ideas aside for a while and come back to them later. And generally, the bigger the issue being tackled, the longer the wait must be before revisiting the ideas. Some of the best creative thinking will come while people are showering, driving, or doing something unrelated to the task at hand—when they aren't *trying* to get ideas.

- ♀ Have an independent panel or committee select the best idea(s), as Starbucks does with their My Starbucks program.

- ♀ If you have hundreds of ideas posted around the room, distribute several dot stickers to each member of the group and have them put them on the ideas that they are excited about (or think have the most potential). Besides looking at all of the ideas that received the most dots, look at the ones that got only a few or none at all, and use those to jump-start your next meeting by building upon them and making them better.

- Once in a while, set up idea competitions to root out the best and the brightest ideas. Wild Idea Clubs shouldn't be based on competition, but if done on occasion for the right reasons, it can instill a healthy sense of sport.

- Some companies implement consumer focus groups or hire a company to manage this for them. Others bring consumers in as part of their session and get immediate feedback on concepts and ideas that were generated only hours, sometimes minutes before. This immediacy can have significant value in honing innovation.

- Organize internal focus groups by gathering people from various departments within your own company and see which ideas excite them. If your idea serves a certain age group or demographic, make sure you include employees who represent it.

- Create an anonymous online survey that offers a small incentive to everyone in the company who completes it. Although some people will only complete the survey to receive the incentive (and therefore will not necessarily contribute serious thought), it's a matter of quantity over quality.

- Use YouTube or e-mail to ask for feedback from everyone in the company (and possibly outside the company, such as customers and clients). This could be in the form of a poll for suggestions. Or, if it seems justified, make it a project that can have far-reaching results. For example, a Wild Idea Club could be set up to fully create a viral video (or more than one) that would be posted online and sent via e-mail. With video cameras and editing software becoming more in reach of the average person (or employee), it's more possible than ever for any employee to produce the company's next big commercial.

❦ Select a hallway that is only used by your company, make sure it is well lit, and create a "gallery" of ideas. (Make sure they are also recorded somewhere else in case they accidentally disappear.) This is a creative way to get additional feedback from more people, create excitement, and build morale. Developed ideas can ultimately stay posted in this gallery, or acknowledged in some way, perhaps in a separate "hall of fame" section.

❦ Do a closing activity at the end of the session, asking members for "one thing they wish your company would move forward on" (of the ideas that had been discussed). This will help get to the best of the best.

❦ Lastly, if the idea isn't proprietary, have club members talk it up with friends and family to get their input. As we've discussed elsewhere in this book, anyone who's an outsider or new to an idea has the potential to see it from a beneficially unique perspective.

STEP 11: PUTTING SOLUTIONS INTO ACTION

It's all well and good to have ideas and decide which is best, but nothing matters until action takes place. Harnessing an idea and putting it into action is like harnessing the wind—large ships traveled across the oceans for centuries on the wind, and great things can happen when ideas are implemented.

Once your club has settled on the idea (or ideas) with which to move forward, it's a good plan to recruit members of the club to serve as an action team. The club can continue to function for further innovation, with this action team being somewhat of a subcommittee, or it may be that the club's purpose has been served and it will now shrink to only include the action team members. (If this happens, however, be sure to regularly keep the former club members apprised on the status of their ideas. Just because they are "out" of the club doesn't mean they should be out of the loop.)

However formed, the action team's sole purpose is to make the idea a reality. The team is almost like a political campaign, in this case working to get an innovation elected. Its functions can be defined as follows:

- Pitch development—As discussed elsewhere (and in more detail in the next step), at some point, decision-makers will be presented with the official idea or ideas that have come from the club. But there's a lot at stake in this step, and so it's crucial to develop and practice the pitch that will be made. Key members of the action team will be responsible for this function.

- Alliances and sponsorship—There is power in numbers and peer influence. An almost necessary component of selling any idea is to show popularity, both in numbers and among opinion leaders. For example, when a Hollywood film is at its earliest stages (being pitched), one of the best things that can be done is to get key people "attached" to it. So, this might mean that Julia Roberts or Will Smith agrees to play the lead, a name director agrees to direct the film, or a reliable financier agrees to put up some money. Whatever the case, the person pitching the film is building alliances to show that the idea is both popular and safe. So, in your corporate situation, this might include getting buy-in from someone in accounting or marketing, or from an external partner, such as a vendor or government agency. Ideally, you'll be seeking the alliances or sponsors who can give you the most pull—who are pulling for you and your club.

💡 Research—Although much research may have been done during the ideation phase, you may find it necessary to do further investigation. For one, as discussed in the next section, it's important to re-search your decision-makers to know what drives and motivates them. But it's also important to re-search how your idea may or will be implemented. The more you can lay the path and show the vi-sion for your idea, the better, and more likely it'll come to be. The Wild Idea Club concept is not just about coming up with ideas, dumping them on someone else, and walking away; it's about making them happen to every degree possible, short of the final decision itself.

💡 Ownership—We strongly advocate giving the in-novating employee or employees ownership in their ideas. That means during ideation, the pitch, and beyond. Recognition and reward are essential, but ownership is the icing on the cake. With this in mind, the action team will include the member(s) who came up with the idea in play. Even if that person has absolutely no capability to do a pitch, form an alliance, or do research (which we strongly doubt), he or she is a vital member of the action team, and ultimately, implementation. It is simply not enough to pat employees on the back, thank them for their ideas, and then run off and make the idea happen. Even if they continue to get recognition for those ideas, nothing can replace their continued involvement in them.

STEP 12: PRESENTING AND PITCHING YOUR IDEAS

There is an art to selling your ideas. Being able to convince others to give you (and your club) the green light and allow you to run with one of your suggestions is both simple and complicated at the same time. It's the blending of all the elements to create a persuasive pitch that makes it an art form. But when it's done right, it's a beautiful thing.

The simple part is the knowledge that those in power (decision-makers in the company) really have only two things in mind when listening to your ideas: One is how the company will benefit, and the other is how it helps the decision-maker—and not necessarily in that order. Basically, the pitch isn't really about you or your idea (as a club); instead it's all about *them*. Once you realize this fact and embrace it, your success rate at selling your ideas will increase dramatically.

You may be saying to yourself, "This idea doesn't really have any inherent value to the company or my boss." Oh, but it does, and this is the art part of the process. How you "spin" your idea to make it match the goals of the organization (and the person you are presenting to) can be very clever, and another thing to brainstorm with the club. Of course, the best ideas usually boost the bottom line, benefit the decision-maker's stature in the company, or improve productivity. Essentially, think money and status. If you can demonstrate a benefit in either area and tie it to a specific decision-maker, then you're in the home stretch.

Other buttons to push to release the resources you need to get your idea off the ground include improving the image and brand of the business, enhancing the work environment so employees are less stressed (which means fewer sick days), and improving motivation and morale (which means they are more enthusiastic about the work to be done and better at their jobs).

But no matter the angle, spin, or decision-maker, every successful pitch will show that the idea is a win-win in some clear way. (The decision-maker and company both win, and your team benefits too.)

Once you nail down the real reasons your idea will be selected, you can move on to some more creative approaches to pitching. But before we go there, let's look at one other vital aspect of selling something up the company ladder—staying on point and staying positive. The Wild Idea Club exists to solve problems, not complain about them, and by keeping the focus on solutions, you will get a lot further than you would by pointing out all the problems and how bad things are. Sure, to solve a problem you need to point out what it is, but spend the bulk of your pitch demonstrating how your idea solves it. One more thing: if you don't believe your idea will work, it will be hard to convince others. Remember, confidence sells, as does passion and excitement. So, the best pitch person will be the one (or ones) who believe in the idea the most.

To help you prepare and deliver the best pitch for your best ideas, here are more techniques and ideas to consider:

💡 The late-night show *Saturday Night Live* is a lot like a Wild Idea Club. The writers come up with sketch ideas and then have to pitch them to the producer to get them on the air. Perhaps your Wild Idea Club can seek a solution through writing and performing a sketch-comedy act that dramatizes the problem and innovation. We're not saying your pitch will be the comedy act (though it could be), but rather that it can help in the creation of your pitch.

💡 Most managers are risk-averse. Show proof that your plan will work and proactively answer or address anticipated objections. Use facts and figure to back up your points, but always remember that people are most engaged by emotions. Use visuals to show and sell. People buy into ideas with their emotions, but will justify making a decision with logic. Lastly, as you'll see in the next point, keep in mind that your logic might not be their logic, and it's *their* logic that ultimately counts.

💡 Know your audience—research and understand to whom you will be "selling" your ideas. Keep in mind that the person who has the final decision may not be in the room when you present and will hear about it secondhand. So, take them into account and ensure that your pitch is easy to convey. Provide the person you're pitching to with take-away items (prototypes, handouts, a PowerPoint presentation) that will help them sell the idea. Lastly, do not make that person do any work. For example, if he or she will need seven copies of your presentation to pass along to a board or committee for approval, *you* make those seven copies. Not only do you want to avoid putting work on that other person, but you also want to make sure everything looks as good as possible.

💡 Know who the "opinion leaders" are—they don't necessarily hold top leadership positions in the company. Find out who they are and gain their support. Who are the key managers? Find out what motivates them and what their pet projects are. Successful ideas are always implemented based on alignment—with the goals of the company and with the goals of the decision-makers (both personally and professionally). Think "alignment = action."

💡 Use negative types to your advantage when developing, preparing, and practicing your pitches. Encourage them to shoot holes in your presentation so you can make it more effective. Take advantage of their "glass is half full" perspective and ask them what is missing. Have them give you all of the reasons your idea won't work and then use the power of the club's innovative capabilities to find solutions.

💡 Keep it as brief as possible. Great ideas often sell themselves, and everyone is short on time. For example, if you have 30 minutes scheduled for the pitch, plan to end at 20 minutes. This will allow time for unexpected delays and decision-maker questions, and if neither occurs, everyone will appreciate a meeting that ran *shorter* than expected (for once) and the extra time they then have.

- If your presentation is high-tech, consider bringing in some of the original charts, drawings, models, collages, and so on. It can be impressive to see the creativity of others, and it adds a human, organic element that is a nice contrast to a highly technical pitch.

STEP 13: REWARDING AND RECOGNIZING YOUR TEAM

Earlier we explored the motivation of managers and how they are looking for ideas that benefit the company as well as themselves. This same principle can be applied in many areas of the workplace. What people crave (besides comfort and compensation) is recognition. And the best part of this is that it doesn't take a lot of time or money to make it happen. People participate in Wild Idea Clubs for a number of reasons, but the biggest benefit may hit a little closer to home—to improve their position in the company and to be acknowledged for their efforts and their ideas. Don't deprive them of this basic need. The following are some of the fundamental principles of employee recognition that need to be incorporated into any Wild Idea Club, but in the true sense of the concept, be sure to come up with some of your own.

- Give credit where credit is due; most people highly value this and appreciate validation. A recent survey of creative types (artists, writers, musicians) found that credit ranked not as far behind compensation as you'd expect, as far as what they most valued. As famed Beatle John Lennon once put it, "I'd rather be rich than famous. That is, slightly more rich and slightly less famous."

♀ Reward your idea people in various ways, with anything and everything from simple thank-you cards to cash rewards. Ideally, these will be tailored to the individuals and what they would most value—what we call "situational rewarding." Whereas most employees put financial incentives first, extra time off and other perks may not be far behind for some people. For example, a working parent whose spouse makes a significant income may appreciate a bonus day of leave to spend with the kids more than a cash bonus. And in many places, parking can be at a premium, so solving an employee's parking problem for a week or month can have a high perceived value. Regardless of the perk, the most important thing is to tie it to the benefit the company has received from the employee's innovation. If the solution generated $100,000 in savings for the company and the employee with the idea received a $10 gift certificate from Applebee's, then something's not right, and further employee ideas will likely dry up. Conversely, a percentage award (percentage of cost-savings goes to the employee) will almost always be well received, if the percentage is fair and generous.

♀ Award shows like the Oscars and Grammys are fun for the viewers, but they are life-changing for the winners. So why not create an "Einstein Award" for the best ideas? Make sure to publicize the winner in your in-house newsletter or communications, and, if appropriate, in public-facing communications such as the company Website. The ultimate award would be to name the product, project, or principal idea after the person (or persons) who came up with it. But whatever the case, people, please come up with something better than the "employee of the month"–style plaques you see on the walls of public waiting areas of restaurants, fast-food places, and hotel lobbies.

Lastly, and perhaps most importantly, reward and recognize your employees' ideas by giving them ownership. This is not meant to be in lieu of a cash award or perk, but in addition to it. If someone has come up with an idea for a program, such as recycling throughout the office, put that person in charge of it. If someone has come up with a purchase of equipment that will save money or increase efficiency, let them oversee that purchase. You get the idea—by giving them ownership, you're giving them the ultimate recognition for their innovation. But what if the person is incapable of being in charge of the idea's implementation? Good question. First, we'd like you to stretch your mind as to whether this is true. Assumptions are often made that an employee lower on the totem pole couldn't run something, but explore that assumption to see if it's really true. What seems to be an incapable employee may just be one who's been unmotivated. If your job were to clean toilets all day, it's hard to be a go-getter. But, given that we're talking about the person who came up with the innovation, and who participated in the Wild Idea Club in the first place, we *are* talking about someone who is at least showing some initiative. Okay, but let's say they are really incapable, for whatever reason. If this is the case, it doesn't mean they don't have a place in the project. It could be that they'll run it, but with the assistance of a mentor or advisor—or, it could be that they'll be the advisor, sitting on a team of employees responsible for the project. Whatever the case, make sure they are at least involved in its implementation. Aside from their ongoing pride of ownership, you may just discover the next rising star in your company.

For more Wild Idea Club tips and a handy checklist, go to *www.WildIdeaClub.com.*

Index

C

D

E

F

About the Authors

LEE SILBER is the award-winning author of 14 books, including the popular "Creative Person" series for Random House. Silber founded a chain of retail stores and now owns a successful corporate-training company, maintaining a busy speaking schedule for clients ranging from Aetna to Wells Fargo. He is a frequent guest on radio and television, and is developing a radio talk show based on the "Wild Idea Club" book. Lee lives with his family in San Diego, California. His Website is *www.leesilber.com*.

ANDREW CHAPMAN has worked in nearly every aspect of independent publishing for more than 20 years. He is an award-winning writer, author of seven books and three audio books, president of Publishers & Writers of San Diego, founder of four companies, and a professional speaker with nearly 300 engagements to his credit throughout the United States and four other countries. Andrew lives in the peaceful and rustic art town of Idyllwild, a mile high in the mountains of Southern California. His Website is *www.achapman.com*.

LINDA KRALL is a strategic illustrator for numerous award-winning package design, branding, and innovation clients. Specializing in ideation sessions, she has brought thousands of ideas to life for global brands, including PepsiCo, GlaxoSmithKline, ConAgra, and other Fortune 500 companies. As a professional facilitator and speaker, Linda leads creativity and innovation workshops. In addition, her work has helped nonprofits raise more than $25 million for various causes. Linda resides in Tustin Ranch, California. Her website is *www.lindakrall.com*.